NORTHERN FRANCE FRANCE NARROW GAUGE

John Organ
Series editor Vic Mitchell

MP Middleton Press

Front cover - Decauville Type Progrès *0-6-0Ts stand at Toury sugar refinery on 27th April1963. This successful class of locomotive was synonymous with the 60cm gauge railways of France. (D.Trevor Rowe).*

Rear cover upper - Réseau Breton Piguet 0-6-6-0T Mallet no. E 417 takes water at Pont Melvez, whilst hauling a mixed train from Guingamp to Carhaix in August 1959. (J.B.Snell).

Rear cover lower - ALCOs reunited. Former TPT no. 3-20, now based at Froissy-Cappy-Dompierre, joins Mountaineer, *formerly 3-23 at Pithiviers, at a Ffestiniog Railway Gala. The two locomotives are seen at Porthmadog prior to double heading a train to Blaenau Ffestiniog on 8th May 1995. (J.F. Organ).*

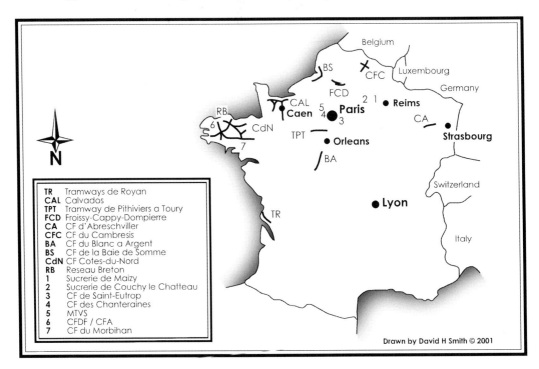

TR   Tramways de Royan
CAL   Calvados
TPT   Tramway de Pithiviers a Toury
FCD   Froissy-Cappy-Dompierre
CA   CF d'Abreschviller
CFC   CF du Cambresis
BA   CF du Blanc a Argent
BS   CF de la Baie de Somme
CdN   CF Cotes-du-Nord
RB   Reseau Breton
1   Sucrerie de Maizy
2   Sucrerie de Couchy le Chatteau
3   CF de Saint-Eutrop
4   CF des Chanteraines
5   MTVS
6   CFDF / CFA
7   CF du Morbihan

Drawn by David H Smith © 2001

Published January 2002

ISBN 1 901706 75 3

© Middleton Press, 2002

Design Deborah Esher

Published by
        Middleton Press
        Easebourne Lane
        Midhurst, West Sussex
        GU29 9AZ
Tel: 01730 813169
Fax: 01730 812601

Printed & bound by Biddles Ltd,
        Guildford and Kings Lynn

CONTENTS

ABBREVIATIONS

ALCO	American Locomotive Corporation
AMTP	Association du Musée des Transports de Pithiviers
APPEVA	L'Association Picarde pour la Preservation et L'Entretien des Vehicules Anciens
CdN	Chemin de Fer des Côtes du Nord
CFC	Chemins de Fer de Calvados
CFCD	Chemin de Fer Touristique Froissy-Cappy-Dompierre
CFD	Chemins de Fer Départementaux
CFTA	Chemins de Fer et des Transport Automobiles
FACS	Fédération des Amis des Chemins de Fer Secondaires
KDL	Kriegs Dampf Lokomotive
SE	Société Général des Chemins de Fer Economiques
TPT	Tramway de Pithiviers à Toury
VFIL	Voies Ferrées d'Intérét Local
WDLR	War Department Light Railways
WW 1	World War 1
WW 2	World War 2

ACKNOWLEDGEMENTS

As usual, this book could not have been completed without the invaluable help of many people. My thanks are due to Monsieur C.Bouchaud, Mr. W.J.K. Davies, Monsieur R.Duton, Dr. R.J. Harley, Dr. J.C.V. Mitchell, Mr. R. Redman, Mr .D. H. Smith, Mr. J.B .Snell, Mr. K. Taylorson, Mr. D. Trevor Rowe, Mr. J.K. Williams and Mrs S.Wright. I must also add a special word of thanks to the Bureau Vaudois d'Adresses (BVA) for their permission to reproduce many of the postcards in their excellent series. Finally, I must thank my wife Brenda, who has once again tolerated my deep involvement in the project. This book was written shortly after a house move and the associated problems. Her support and encouragement in such difficult circumstances are doubly appreciated.

INTRODUCTION

As recorded in the companion volume to this book *Southern France Narrow Gauge*, France ultimately boasted over 17000 miles of local railways throughout the country. Following the passing in 1865 of a law known as *Loi Migneret*, authorising the construction of local railways and a subsequent act in 1880 (*Le Plan Freycinet)*, construction began in earnest. Secondary lines were constructed either as standard, metre or 60cm gauges, depending upon the terrain of the area and the finance available. There were two categories of railway, *Intérét Général* and *Intérét Local.* The former were the larger and more extensive systems which were controlled by the State whilst the latter were the smaller operations which were the responsibility of the respective département.

Unlike Southern France, which relied mainly on extensive metre gauge systems in the mountainous regions of the Massif Central, Alps and Pyrénées, Northern France had numerous short lines, many of them 60cm. Unlike the rugged terrain in the South, the lines in the North traversed mainly flat and featureless landscapes with very little in the way of notable heavy civil engineering structures. There were exceptions, the extensive metre gauge systems in Brittany being a notable example. So numerous were the lines in the area, it would be impossible to cover them all in detail. Consequently, this book will look at a selection of the more important systems, including some which have survived. These survivors are largely only part of the original lines, in some cases very small sections. They, of course, cater mainly for the tourist industry rather than their original function of conveying passengers and goods as a means of transport in the area of their operations.

With a lack of heavy gradients and excessive curvature, smaller locomotives were obviously normally employed. However, a huge variety of machinery was to be seen during the heyday of these interesting railways. 0-6-0Ts and 2-6-0Ts were the usual motive power on the metre gauge systems whilst small 0-4-2Ts and 0-6-0Ts were more common on the 60cm lines. Again Brittany was the major exception. With heavy trains running through a more rugged area on its extensive system, the Réseau Breton operated a fleet of large 0-6-6-0T Mallets for its freight trains and some very useful 4-6-0Ts for passenger trains. The 60cm lines received a legacy of WW 1 when many surplus locomotives from the military lines of both sides of the conflict became available. As in other parts of France, railcars took over many of the passenger workings from the 1930s with vehicles from De Dion, Billard, Renault and SCF-Verney becoming a common sight. Once again the Réseau Breton had the largest units when they inherited some impressive Decauville machines as a result of a cancelled export order.

The only notable metre gauge lines in Northern France to survive are the Chemin de Fer du Baie de Somme with its two branches running each side of the Somme estuary, and part of the Le Blanc-Argent system. Even the mighty Réseau Breton succumbed to inevitable closure in 1967, although one branch survived having been converted to standard gauge. Three principal lines of the smaller gauges have formed the basis of successful tourist and museum operations. A small section of the Tramway de Pithiviers à Toury was one of the pioneers of railway preservation in France, whilst the Froissy-Cappy-Dompierre line is a lasting tribute to the military supply lines of WW 1. The other important tourist railway is to be found in Alsace, where part of the 70cm CF Forestier D'Abreschviller continues to operate. Sadly, lines such as the Côtes du Nord and CF du Cambrésis are now just a distant memory although fortunately some of their equipment has survived elsewhere.

The erecting shop of the Decauville Works at Corbel is seen during the early years of the 20th century. In the foreground are 0-4-0Ts in various stages of construction. (Coll. R.Duton).

1. DECAUVILLE AND THE 60cm GAUGE

When describing the Narrow Gauge railways of France, particularly those of 60cm gauge, one name will always figure prominently. Paul Decauville (1846-1922) was born into a farming family at Petit-Bourg, near Paris. By 1864 Paul had taken over control of the farming business, which by that time had been expanded to include an engineering workshop constructing sugar refining machinery for the numerous distilleries in the area around Paris. In 1870 the engineering business was also constructing farm machinery including stationary steam engines.

Aware of the difficulties that farmers were having with their horse drawn wagons being bogged down in the fields during the sugar beet harvesting period, a system of portable railway track was designed and constructed for use in the fields which was an instant success. Initially the wagons were either horse drawn or hand propelled and the application was adapted for other forms of industry such as quarries and brick works. Inspired by the success of locomotive hauled narrow gauge railways, such as the Ffestiniog and Penrhyn in North Wales, which proved that a small locomotive could successfully haul trains on a gauge as small as 2ft (60cm), the logical development was to adapt these portable rail systems to locomotive haulage.

Initially in 1878, machines designed by Decauville were built by the Paris firm of Le.Corpet, and the Belgian Couillet Company. Before long the Petit-Bourg works were building locomotives in addition to track sections and associated equipment. Orders were soon being received from far and wide for complete portable railway systems including locomotives and wagons. The small 0-4-0T and 0-6-0T machines were joined by more complex 0-4-4-0T Mallets, designed by another Belgian concern, *SA la Metallurgique* at Tubize. However, it is for the basic smaller locomotives that Decauville is best remembered. The original 0-4-0T diminutive Type 1 and Type 3 locomotives built at Petit-Bourg were ultimately developed into the familiar *Type Progrès* introduced in 1911, construction continuing over many years as both 0-4-0T (Five Tonne) and 0-6-0T (Nine Tonne) machines. These were the most characteristic Decauville design with their rectangular side tanks and curved profile of their cab roofs. Prior to the latter designs, a successful range of Type 10 (Ten Tonne) 0-6-2Ts had been introduced in 1897, similar in design to the Seven Tonne 0-4-2Ts built by Weidknecht. Between 1908 and 1914 many Decauville locomotives were built under licence by Borsig of Berlin in their capacity of agents. These were constructed for use on various gauges of track, the 60cm examples all being 0-4-0Ts. In 1915, a number of the 0-6-0T *Type Progrès* machines were built by Kerr Stuart in Stoke-on-Trent to the order of the French military railway department. These were known as the *Joffre* class by their builders, many of them returning to this country in later years for preservation.

In 1887 *Société Decauville Aîné* supplied the equipment for a short 60cm passenger carrying line from La Baule to Le Pouliguen but two years later this enterprise was to be eclipsed by a 3km line laid to serve the Paris Exhibition of 1889. The line ran from the Place de la Concorde to the Eiffel Tower, which would have necessitated crossing the Seine. During its six months of operation the line, with a fleet of five Tubize Mallets and Decauville bogie coaches, conveyed over 6,000,000 passengers with a daily average of more than 35,000 - a remarkable figure by any standard. This success, more than anything else, vindicated the suitability of the 60cm gauge for passenger carrying lines in areas where the larger gauges were unsuitable. The smaller gauge was ideally suited for roadside tramways, which were cheap to construct and operate. With this increase in the engineering side of the business, a second factory was opened at Corbeil, which ultimately took over most of the locomotive production from Petit-Bourg. In December 1889 the company name was changed to *Société des Etablissements Decauville Aîné* and entered into an agreement with the Paris based firm of *F.Weidknecht et Compagnie* to construct some of the orders.

As a result of the success of the Paris Exhibition line, many local authorities showed interest in adopting 60cm gauge for local tramways whilst in three cases Decauville tendered successfully to construct and operate complete local systems. These were from the municipality of Royan (1890), the Département of Calvados (1891) and the Département of Loiret for a line linking Pithiviers and Toury in 1892. The three systems were all very different in character with equally different results.

Unfortunately the *Société des Etablissements Decauville Aîné* was not as efficient at operating railways as it was as building them and the ultimate destiny of these systems is now described. However, the Tramway de Pithiviers à Toury enjoyed a longer and rather more successful life than its contemporaries and therefore deserves a separate chapter.

Tramways de Royan

Strictly speaking the resort of Royan, which is situated in the west of France on the north side of the Gironde estuary, is not in Northern France and therefore does not really qualify for inclusion in this book. However it is included for completeness of the Decauville connection. The concession, for building and operating the line, was instigated by the Mayor of Royan on a municipal basis. Having been impressed by the Paris Exhibition line, the Mayor suggested to Paul Decauville that Royan would be an ideal location for a similar operation. In return, Decauville was looking for a suitable location to utilise the stock and equipment from the exhibition line. Consequently

Decauville promptly agreed with the Mayor's proposal and in February 1890 began serious discussions with the council. Following the usual suggestions and amendments, agreement was reached for a 50 -year concession to lay and operate a 60cm gauge track alongside existing public roads and verges.

Hardly had the ink dried on the contract and construction began on the initial 5.0km. section from the Champ de Foire, near the beach, to Foncillon on the outskirts of Royan. Even in 1890, Royan was a busy seaside town and much opposition was heard from many quarters when the tramway was built along the congested main street. Undaunted by the protests, the line was extended at both ends during the summer of the same year. From Foncillon it continued a further 1.3 km. to La Falaise which opened on 10th August. On 15th June 1891 the line was extended a further 0.5 km. to its final terminus at Pontaillac, following the construction of a stone embankment which cut off a corner of the beach and produced more howls of protest! Meanwhile in Royan itself, the line was extended in stages. Initially a 0.5km section to the Grand Hotel was opened on the same day as the Foncillon line, which was ultimately extended a further 3.0km. to St.Georges de Didonne, the final stretch opening on 28th June 1891. There was also a short branch from the Champ de Foire to the ETAT station at Royan. This had a very short life as most potential passengers found it easier to walk from the main line terminus to the town centre.

As mentioned above, the Decauville Company was to be less efficient at operating railways as it was at building the equipment to run on them. The original company went into liquidation in August 1893. The reformed company known as the *Société des Anciens Etablissements Decauville Aîné*, without Paul Decauville at its head, concentrated on its successful business as a manufacturer. Meanwhile the concession to operate the Tramway de Royan, which had been declared a Public Utility, was transferred to a new company formed by local prominent businessmen (including some Decauville shareholders) and councillors and known as the *Société Général des Tramways de Royan*. Having taken control of the tramway, the new operators decided to extend the line still further. A 6.50km. extension along the coast from Pontaillac to La Grande Côte was opened by Easter 1897, the extension actually being operated by a subsidiary company known as the *Société du Tramway de la Grande Côte a Royan*. This section of the line abandoned its roadside formation and took a route through the sand dunes, with some fairly steep gradients to surmount. A further extension was constructed at the eastern end of the system where a 2.0km branch ran alongside the road from St Georges Port to Le Paradou.

The Tramways de Royan were not affected to a great extent by WW 1, their only contribution to the war effort being some transporting of timber for various defence works along the coast. In 1924 the line was extended yet again in a rather different manner. Since the mid 19th century a metre gauge line known as the Tramway Forestier had operated north from La Grande Côte, through the forest that bordered the coast, to Ronce les Baines on the estuary of the River Seudre, a distance of 27km. An agreement was drawn up for an 18-year concession in which the *Société Général des Tramways de Royan* would take over operation of the Tramway Foristier and convert the latter to 60cm. Although a link between the two lines was built at La Grande Côte, they continued to be operated separately, the connecting line only being used for the transfer of stock.

Although the traffic figures of the halcyon days of the Decauville period, when over 350,000 passengers were carried during the season, never returned, the enlarged system continued to provide a largely seasonal service until WW 2 and the German occupation. The concession was due to expire in 1944, but was extended in order that the occupying forces could continue to use the line in conjunction with its coastal defences. By that time, the locomotives, rolling stock and infrastructure were in a run down state and closure was inevitable once peace was declared. However, the heavy bombardment of the Royan area during the early months of 1945 destroyed much of the track and rolling stock, which effectively resolved the matter. The locomotives and infrastructure that did survive were scrapped in 1948, which sadly consigned the Tramways de Royan to history.

Locomotives and Rolling Stock

The first locomotives to work at Royan in 1890 were four, Tubize built 0-4-4-0T Mallets that had worked at the Paris Exhibition. In addition a Decauville Three Tonne 0-4-0T was used for construction work on the various sections of the line. In 1891, three of the Mallets were transferred to the Calvados system whilst Royan received eight 0-4-2Ts built by Weidknecht. The fate of the surviving Mallet at Royan is uncertain. The Weidknecht 0-4-2Ts were joined in 1898 by three Decauville 10 Tonne 0-6-2Ts, the type 10s being known subsequently by the unofficial name of *Type Royan* although their use wasn't confined to that line. In 1907 one of the 0-6-2Ts was sold to an industrial line in Var, being replaced by a further 0-4-2T. This final addition to the locomotive stock had a slightly heavier axle load than the earlier machines and was distinguishable by its longer side tanks with sloping tops. All the Royan locomotives sported large conical spark arresting chimneys in deference to the dry terrain of much of the route.

The Tramway Forestier had used some primitive petrol engine tramcars during its earlier metre gauge period. This use of self propelled machines continued following its incorporation into the Tramways de Royan. Six railcars built by *Entrepise Campagne* were provided for the service. These four -wheeled vehicles had open sides protected by side curtains and wooden cross bench seats for 25 passengers. The final two were slightly superior, being fitted with upholstered seats but with a reduced capacity of 21 passengers. Despite their primitive design, they did have the advantage of a driving position at each end.

The locomotive hauled trains were formed from a fleet of standard Decauville type KE bogie coaches. These were open sided, with curtains to protect the passengers from inclement weather, and wooden "toast rack" seating with a capacity of 48. A maximum of 32 of these coaches operated on the line, although only about 25 were available for service at any time. At various times, some of the vehicles were rebuilt with new open sided bodies whilst four of the coaches were completely reconstructed into a pair of high capacity centre entrance vehicles. As freight traffic on the line was virtually non existent, the only goods vehicles were a four-wheeled van and some tipper wagons used mainly for track maintenance work.

Tramways de Calvados

The situation in the Normandy region of Calvados, with some developing holiday resorts, was slightly different to that at Royan. The département had been considering inviting tenders for a metre gauge network for some time and had in fact accepted a proposal from the *Groupe Empain* for such a system. However the upsurge in interest for 60cm lines after 1889 resulted in a rethink by the département and the *Groupe Empain* were asked to submit a revised tender based on the smaller gauge, which they declined. With the successful Paris Exhibition line influencing the councillors, an approach was made to Paul Decauville to construct a similar line to that currently under construction at Royan. Once again, this was an ideal situation for Decauville who was able to utilise more of the equipment made redundant following the closure of the Paris line.

Initially two separate lines were proposed. One was a mainly coastal 29km route from Dives to Luc-sur-Mer with a short inland diversion in order to cross the River Orne and its adjacent canal between Ranville and Benouville. The coast was regained at Ouistreham for the remaining 9km to Luc-sur-Mer. The other line was in the west of the département connecting Isigny to Grandcamp-les-Bains, a distance of 10km.

Construction of the Dives to Luc-sur-Mer line was begun before both lines were declared to be of Public Utility on 5th September 1891, the concession with Decauville having been signed in October 1890. Consequently the Ouistreham to Luc-sur-Mer section began operations on 15th August 1891 with an official opening on 15th October. The eastern arm from Dives was opened as far as Sallenelles on 15th July 1892 with the final link to Ouistreham on 24th August following completion of the two swing bridges at Ranville and Benouville. The bridge at Ranville, which enabled the line to cross the River Orne, was designed by Gustave Eiffel. On 4th July 1893, a 7km branch from Benouville

along the side of the canal to the basin at Caen was opened, having been delayed by the financial state of the *Société Decauville.* This situation also delayed the construction of the Isigny to Grandcamp line.

Following the demise of the *Société Decauville* in its original manifestation, a new concessionaire was required in order for the Calvados system to remain in business, and expand its routes as intended. The result was the concession being granted to associates of the *Groupe Empain* who originally had declined to be involved with a 60cm gauge railway. Consequently the concession was transferred to *Société Anonyme des Chemins de Fer de Calvados* (CFC) on 1st August 1895.

Despite the reluctant use of 60cm gauge, the CFC began its expansion programme by adopting metre gauge principals such as 18kg rail on wooden sleepers rather than the 15kg Vignoles rails laid on steel sleepers as favoured by Decauville. However, the new routes continued to be laid largely as roadside tramways apart from areas where deviations had to be made to avoid excessive gradients. In addition Westinghouse continuous braking was adopted for all stock, a technical leap forward for a 60cm line at that time.

As mentioned above, construction of the line from Isigny to Grandcamp had been delayed by the financial problems of the old Decauville concern. No sooner had the CFC inherited the concession, a start was made on construction of this isolated 10km line which opened on 27th July 1896. Two Tubize locomotives, a Mallet and a 0-6-0T, were supplied to operate the line. The former was transferred from the original section whilst the latter was supplied new. On 15th June 1897, authorisation was given for more lines throughout the département to be constructed. These comprised of sections connecting Grandcamp to Molay de Littry (32km), Courseulles to Bayeux (26km) which also included a short branch to Arromanches, Caen to Falaise (45km) and Bayeux to Port-en-Bessin (11km). In addition the branch from Ouistreham to Caen canal basin was extended the short distance to St.Pierre in 1898 in order to connect with the Falaise line. The various sections were opened between 1899, with the lines radiating from Bayeux, and 1902 when the Falaise line was finally opened on 20th September, following delays incurred whilst agreeing the route. On 18th January 1904, this line was extended at its southern end from Falaise-Château to the main line station at Falaise Gare. Between 1904 and 1906 further extensions were added to the system. A 9.5km line from Molay de Littry to Balleroy was built to connect with a line from Bayeux to St.Martin des Besaces (40.5km).

With the two major sections of the system effectively isolated from each other, it was obvious that they should be connected at the earliest opportunity. This had been largely achieved by laying a third rail along the standard gauge CF de Caen a la Mer for 10km between Luc-sur-Mer and Courseulles. The interlaced lines separated at St.Aubin-sur-Mer in order to provide a passing loop for both gauges. With this connection, which had been opened on 1st July 1900, it allowed for some rationalisation of locomotives and rolling stock. One major benefit was the establishment of a main works and depot at Caen Demi-Lune, which was developed into a fairly large complex. The total mileage of the CFC, including various small branches and extensions at Caen and Falaise, eventually reached a quite staggering 234km. Various ambitious plans were suggested during the first decade of the 20th century for even more extensions which would, had they borne fruit, added a further 369km. With a fairly extensive standard gauge system throughout most of the département, and an improving road system, it was not surprising that these schemes were abandoned as being unnecessary.

Although the original coastal routes carried sufficient traffic during the years prior to WW 1 to provide favourable financial returns, the same could certainly not be said of the inland extensions. It was argued that had the system been constructed in metre gauge, which would not have cost much more, there would have been more opportunity to provide a competitive service throughout the département. Despite the introduction of railcars during the 1920s, it was still an uphill battle to compete with an increasing bus service. It was, therefore, no surprise when the first closure took place in 1929. This was at the western end of the system when the line from Isigny to Balleroy closed on December 2nd of that year. This was closely followed by the lines radiating from Bayeux which all closed between 1930 and 1933 together with the Caen to Falaise section, which closed in 1930. Even the more successful coastal route didn't escape the onslaught when the line from Benouville to Dives was transferred to bus operation in 1932. In fact this particular closure was for a slightly different reason. The swing bridge across the canal at Benouville was in need of replacement with the consequent installation of a lifting bridge in its place. It was decided to be not economically viable to lay tracks on the new structure in view of the limited life expectancy of the CFC system. This replacement lifting bridge, in conjunction with its neighbouring river bridge at Ranville, was to earn its place in history during the night of 5th / 6th June 1944. Six Horsa gliders, containing D Company of 6th Airborne Division, landed alongside the two bridges, the first allied troops to arrive in Normandy. Since that historic night, the lifting bridge at Benouville has been known as "Pegasus Bridge", the name being perpetuated even today for the modern replacement installed in 1994.

Locomotives and Rolling Stock

The initial locomotives supplied for use on the Tramways du Calvados in 1891 where five Tubize 0-4-4-0T Mallets, three of which were transferred from Royan. During 1892/3, two similar locomotives constructed by Decauville at Petit Bourg were added

to the roster. The "odd man out" supplied to the original company was a Weidknecht 0-6-2T, which was delivered in 1892.

Following the transfer of the concession to the CFC, the locomotive stock was enlarged by an influx of more conventional machines, the Mallets all being sold by 1908. The first of the new locomotives was a 0-6-0T built by Blanc-Misseron for Tubize in 1895. Six similar machines from the same manufacturer arrived in 1899/1900, these differing from the 1895 example in being fitted with twin cabs (bi-cabines), in view of the tramway nature of the system, referred to as 0-6-0TR to distinguish them from the earlier locomotive. Blanc-Misseron next supplied a pair of 0-6-4TRs in 1901 for use on the Falaise line, basically 0-6-0TRs with longer frames and a rear bogie to aid stability. The most notable locomotives supplied to the CFC were the sixteen 4-6-0TR and 4-6-0Ts supplied between 1902 and 1909. Six of these machines were conventional 4-6-0Ts supplied by Weidknecht for use on the Luc-sur-Mer - Caen - Dives section. The other ten were further products of Blanc-Misseron / Tubize and were 4-6-0TR twin cab variants for use on the various inland sections of the system. Finally in 1913, Tubize supplied three 0-6-2TRs for use on the Falaise line. Their intended purpose was for projected mineral traffic, which never materialised.

In an attempt to economise the operation of the service, three Crochat four wheeled railcars were supplied in 1925. These were powered by two electric motors driven by a 30hp petrol engine, and were equipped with Westinghouse brakes and dual driving positions. Seating capacity was 13 with provision for a further 15 standing passengers. In 1936 they were joined by two, second-hand, Decauville railcars. These were more powerful variants fitted with four electric motors connected to two bogies. Seating capacity was 19 plus a baggage compartment, but had the disadvantage of being single ended which rendered them less versatile than the earlier vehicles. After closure of the CFC, the two Decauville railcars were transferred to Pithiviers whilst the three Crochat variants were scrapped.

The original coaches were a fleet of standard Decauville KE type bogie "toast rack" vehicles similar to those supplied to Royan. With the anticipated increase in service additional coaches, of an improved design, were supplied by Decauville. The KG type were described as semi-open having wooden vertical planking bodywork with open elliptical openings above the waist. The final development was the classic Decauville coach design, designated IS type, which were fully glazed wooden bodied bogie coaches, with end balconies and entrances. All these had a seating capacity of 48, the final design being either 1st / 2nd class or 2nd / 3rd class composites, or 3rd class / luggage variants. During the CFC era, the original bogie coaches were joined by a total of 80, Belgian built, four wheeled vehicles. These were supplied in various combinations of 1st, 2nd and 3rd class accommodation with a seating capacity of 16 in the closed vehicles and 24 in the open "toast rack" variants. They were certainly far inferior to the later Decauville design but had the obvious advantage of being cheap to acquire.

With a limited amount of freight traffic on the Calvados system, goods wagons were mainly four-wheeled open stock with a capacity of 10 tonnes. For the anticipated mineral traffic, a number of steel bodied lowside wagons, including ten bogie variants, were supplied by Decauville. Due to the lack of suitable traffic, these vehicles never achieved their full potential.

The finale of the CFC

As recorded above, after 1932 the only section of the system to remain in operation was the line from Caen to Luc-sur-Mer, via Ouistreham. During the 1930s this mainly coastal route operated a summer only service. Following the outbreak of WW 2, this was increased to an all year operation with a minimum of two trains daily. The route from Ouistreham to Luc-sur- Mer ran along the coast, this area of coast line being better known in history as "Sword" beach following the D-Day landings of 6th June 1944. At about 7.50am on that historic date, the first train of the day was about to depart from the small station at Luc-sur-Mer. However, at about the same time the first flotilla of landing craft containing the British troops were heading for "Sword" beach whilst a bombardment of naval shells were being aimed at the coastal defences. Needless to say the train was hastily abandoned, its fate unknown. Within hours the area had been overrun with amphibious Sherman tanks which had no respect for the lightly laid narrow gauge railway track which lay in their path. With one momentous historical event gaining momentum, the Chemins de Fer de Calvados finally expired in one of the most dramatic closures of any railway.

CF de Calvados

Not to Scale

Drawn by David H Smith © 2001

1 Ouistreham
2 Benouville
3 Ranville

1.1.   A short lived 60cm line was constructed between 1899 and 1903 to Decauville principles   connecting Quend, near Le Touquet, with the resorts of Quend-Plage and Fort Mahon. This view shows the scene at Fourriel, where the two lines bisected.   (Coll. R. Harley).

1.2.   A panoramic overhead view of the promenade at Royan shows the close proximity of the tramway to the beach and rough seas of the Atlantic coast. (Coll. R. Harley).

1.3.   A Weidknecht built locomotive hauls a train through the forest section of the Tramways de Royan. The large spark arresting chimney is clearly shown in this view. (Coll. J.K.Williams).

1.4.   Weidknecht 4-6-0T no.13 waits at Ouistreham on the Chemin de Fer de Calvados during the 1920s. This location is near the present day Ferry Port, which is to the right beyond the bridge over the canal in the foreground. (Coll. J.K.Williams).

1.5.   A train from Luc-sur-Mer arrives at Ouistreham (Riva-Bella) along the Route de Lion. The photograph is undated but the dress of the bystanders suggests it was taken during the 1930s.   (Coll. W.J.K Davies).

1.6.   Blanc-Misseron 4-6-0TR no.106 departs from Courseulles with a train bound for Bayeux. The CFC used the existing roads as much as possible for its various routes. (Coll. FACS).

1.7.   A Decauville Mallet hauls a train across the Gustave Eiffel designed swing bridge spanning the River Orne at Ranville. The rolling stock consists of Decauville IS type bogie coaches and Belgian built four wheeled vehicles. (Coll. FACS).

1.8.   Works photograph of Blanc-Misseron 4-6-0TR "bi-cabine" no.102. Ten of these locomotives were supplied between 1902 and 1909. (Coll. FACS).

2. TRAMWAY DE PITHIVIERS À TOURY

Unlike the original schemes at Royan and Calvados, the situation in the Département du Loiret was rather different. The two principal towns of Pithiviers and Toury, 31km apart, were separated by a flat landscape of farmland and poor roads. Sugar beet was one of the principal crops grown in the area. Both towns had important sugar refineries and were served by the standard gauge railway network, Toury being situated on the main P.O. route from Paris to Orléans. However, the département realised that a suitable light railway system linking the many isolated farms and villages with the two towns would be a major benefit to the area. Once again, the Decauville principles of 60cm gauge appeared to be the perfect answer. The portable lightweight track would be invaluable for the many branches leading into the fields during the sugar beet harvesting period.

A concession for 15 years was agreed with the Société Decauville in August 1891, with construction starting the following month. The majority of the Tramway de Pithiviers à Toury (TPT) was completed the following year and was opened from Pithiviers to a temporary terminus at Toury on 25th July 1892. Ultimately the line was extended with a level crossing over the P.O. line to a new terminus alongside the standard gauge station. A connection with the internal rail system at the Toury sugar refinery was also laid from this station. Due to complications in constructing this crossing and the new station layout, this short extension did not open until early in 1894.

At Pithiviers, a large workshop and locomotive shed complex was built alongside the station whilst, as at Toury, rail connections were laid to the refinery. This workshop was fully equipped and capable of carrying out all kinds of maintenance from minor overhauls to major rebuilds. The route was largely built alongside the existing roads, which at that time were of poor standard and in many cases were nothing more than dirt tracks. Some deviations were made away from the roads in order to pass behind the small villages and hamlets that can be seen for miles across the windswept plains. The country stations, many of which still survive as farm buildings, were substantially built wooden affairs, incorporating a goods shed, booking office and waiting room under one large roof. At these stations, sidings sprouted from the "main line" into the fields to facilitate the loading of sugar beet during the harvesting periods. The route passed through many locations with similar names just to confuse the issue! The principal stations were at Guigneville (7km), Greneville (12km), Chatillon le Roi (15km), Izy (17km), Bazoches-les-Gallerandes (19.5km) and Outarville (25km), all distances quoted are from Pithiviers. In addition a number of halts were provided at Ormes, Bitry, Torville, Moulin-de-Grenville, Landreville, Gendreville, Arcanville, Brendelon and Germonville.

Both sugar refineries at each end of the line had their own internal tramway systems with a small fleet of locomotives and wagons. The refinery lines interlaced with the TPT before branching off across the fields in much the same way as the branches from the "main line" did. The Toury refinery line remained independent until 1964 unlike the Pithiviers refinery system, which was closed in the late 1950s with most of its equipment absorbed by the TPT.

Predominantly a freight line, carrying milk and other agricultural merchandise in addition to sugar beet, a limited passenger service was operated until 1951. Originally three trains in each direction daily, this was reduced to a twice daily service during WW 2 which remained until withdrawal of the passenger service. In comparison the freight operations were very intensive, especially during the harvest periods, with an extensive and varied stock of locomotives and rolling stock available.

In much the same way as its contemporaries at Royan and Calvados, the TPT was to be affected by the failure of the original Decauville concern. As a result the concession was terminated and the railway transferred to the Département du Loiret on 1st January 1899. The département duly transferred the operation of the line to its *Ponts et Chaussees* (Bridges and Roads) department who assumed control on 29th March 1901. The freight traffic continued to grow necessitating the need to acquire extra locomotives and rolling stock. The first of four railcars arrived for passenger use in 1922 followed by a second in 1926. Finally in 1937 the two railcars, previously mentioned, arrived from the CFC by which time the majority of passenger workings were operated by internal combustion machines. As will be explained in the relevant section, the locomotive stock was expanded with additions from numerous sources. Many came from the WW 1 field railways from both sides of the conflict whilst the final arrivals in 1945/6 were four unused powerful machines ordered by the occupying German forces during WW 2 for their military supply lines.

Traffic continued to be profitable, especially during the harvest periods, until the 1940s. Following WW 2, the improved roads and increase in road traffic began to make inroads into the TPTs receipts. The passenger service was withdrawn in 1951 but it continued to operate freight trains despite fighting an uphill battle with road transport for a further decade. The TPT eventually closed in December 1964 although a special for enthusiasts was run on 22nd May 1965, such was the interest in the line. However, as will be seen later, this was not the end of the Pithiviers story.

Locomotives and Rolling Stock

A total of 35 locomotives were acquired for use

on the TPT during its 72 years existence. Many were acquired second hand from a variety of sources whilst some of the earlier arrivals were withdrawn at various times, being replaced by later machines. During the sugar beet harvesting period, when the railway was at its busiest, at least 15 locomotives would be in steam during a normal day's operation. The stock included examples of French, British, German and American, with a wide range of wheel arrangements including 0-4-2T, 0-6-0T, 4-6-0T, 2-6-2T, 0-8-0T and 0-10-0T, plus 0-4-4-0T and 0-6-6-0T Mallets. Due to this varied stock of machines, the TPT devised a unique numbering system. Each locomotive had its individual number, which was prefixed by another indicating the number of driven axles. Hence a 0-6-0T would be, for example, 3-6, a 0-8-0T example 4-12, whilst a 0-10-0T would be 5-3. In the case of the Mallets, a 0-4-4-0T could be 22-5 whilst the sole 0-6-6-0T was 33-1.

During the period of the Decauville concession, not surprisingly Petit Bourg supplied the first locomotives between 1892 and 1894. These were a pair of 0-4-4-0T Mallets and three 0-4-2Ts. One of the latter was, in fact, a product of Weidknecht, which proved to be unsatisfactory in service. Consequently it was returned to Paris and exchanged for another similar machine built at Petit Bourg. Following the transfer of the operating concession to the Département in 1901 the five original locomotives were joined by three Decauville 0-6-0Ts (Nos. 3-1 to 3-3), with another similar second hand example (3-4) arriving in 1925. At around the same time, one of the 0-4-2Ts was exchanged for a Blanc-Misseron 0-6-0T (3-5) built in 1902.

The two original Decauville Mallets (22-3 and 22-4) were joined in 1929 by a similar locomotive, which was transferred from Calvados, and allocated the number 22-2. Meanwhile four larger machines of the same wheel arrangement built by Orenstein and Koppel in 1905 (22-1 and 22-5 to 22-7) were acquired from various sources between 1917 and 1930. The unique 0-6-6-0 was built in 1916 by Decauville, as part of a large order for military use in Morocco. For some reason one locomotive remained in France and eventually arrived at Pithiviers in 1923. Originally a tender engine, it was converted to a 0-6-6-0T by fitting rather ungainly side tanks and became No. 33-1. The tender was utilised as a reserve water vehicle.

Following World War 1, a large number of surplus locomotives from the field railways of both sides of the conflict became available. Some of these had seen very little use before being acquired by dealers who promptly sold them to many 60cm systems throughout France. Consequently, in the 1920s the TPT acquired five of the familiar "Feldbahn" 0-8-0Ts, which were built to a standard design by the major German manufacturers. The examples at the TPT were products of Humboldt, Schwartzkopff, Henschel and Krauss, dating from 1916-18. They acquired the numbers 4-1 to 4-5 and replaced some of the earlier

locomotives. In addition to the "Feldbahns", six locomotives from the Allied side of the war effort arrived during the same period. These included two former W.D Hunslet 4-6-0Ts (3-10 and 3-11) and four ALCO 2-6-2Ts (3-20 to 3-23). The latter had remained at the premises of a dealer for over a decade before being sold to the TPT between 1931 and 1934.

The sugar refinery at Pithiviers had inherited three German 0-10-0Ts during the 1920s, which were basically enlarged versions of the "Feldbahns". Products of Borsig, Schwartzkopff and O & K in 1917, they were transferred to the TPT between 1927 and 1939 acquiring the numbers 5-1 to 5-3 respectively. At the time, these were the largest and most powerful locomotives on the system. However in 1945 a number of unused Franco-Belge 0-8-0s ordered by the German occupying forces became available. These powerful machines were built to a standard design in a variety of gauges (a 75cm example from Austria survives on the Welshpool and Llanfair Railway) and the TPT acquired four 60cm examples. Known as Type KDL (*Kriegs Dampf Lokomotive*), they were originally constructed as tender / tank locomotives. The examples supplied to Pithiviers, and those to other 60cm lines in France, were converted to 0-8-0Ts. The tenders were replaced by additional side tanks, situated in front of the original short tanks. These additional tanks extended beyond the smokebox and were supported by a cradle attached to the front of the frames. The result was a very powerful, albeit not very attractive, locomotive. The KDLs became the mainstay of the operation during the final years of the TPT, allowing more of the older machines to be retired. Their numbers were 4-10 to 4-13. In 1962, two similar locomotives (4-14 and 4-15) were inherited from the recently closed sugar refinery at Coucy. These final additions to the stock never ran on the TPT, being used as a source of spare parts for their hard working sisters.

As previously mentioned, railcars made an appearance during the 1920s for some of the lighter passenger workings. In 1922 a Crochat petrol-electric four-wheeled vehicle was put into service. A single ended version, it had a seating capacity of 30 and towed a small luggage van if it was deemed necessary. Franco-Belge supplied a 48 seat version with mechanical transmission in 1926 which allowed for virtually all the passenger trains to be operated by railcars. Following closure of the Calvados system in 1944, two Decauville bogie railcars built in 1936 were transferred to the TPT as recorded in the previous chapter.

Being predominantly a freight operation, the stock of passenger coaches was rather minimal. Six Decauville fully closed end balcony bogie coaches (type IS) were supplied during the period of the Decauville concession, along with three "fourgons". Between 1931 and 1939, five of the coaches were rebuilt with central double doors and the end balconies removed. These rebuilds were designated as V1 to V5. This remained the total passenger stock until 1942 when an additional bogie coach was constructed in the workshop at Pithiviers to the same design and given the number V6.

The goods stock consisted of a huge number of open wagons used for transporting sugar beet together with some closed vans and cattle trucks. The initial vehicles were Decauville products, which were joined later by many built in the versatile workshops at Pithiviers and Toury. The freight wagons were a mixture of four wheeled and bogie types, the high capacity bogie wagons being of great use during the busy sugar beet harvesting periods.

Musée des Transports de Pithiviers

As previously mentioned, the closure of the TPT was not the end of the line. In 1962 a number of enthusiasts in the Lyon area, with the indefatigable Jean Arrivetz at their lead, had been aware of the rapidly diminishing 60cm lines throughout France. In an attempt to save something of their heritage they had established a short line on a new site near Lyon and collected suitable equipment to operate it. Known as the CF Touristique de Meyzieu, one of the first locomotives to be acquired was the O & K Mallet number 22-5. Following the closure of the TPT, the Mallet was joined by one of the Franco-Belge 0-8-0Ts, 4-13.

Of course, the Meyzieu line was not a preserved railway in the true sense, but a valiant attempt to save some of the historic locomotives and rolling stock that were rapidly being scrapped. As soon as the TPT closed, a serious attempt was made to save at least part of this historic railway. Discussions began immediately for the possibility of preserving part of the line for posterity, the first example of its kind in France. Pithiviers was chosen in view of its large workshop, depot and station area. In addition the 3.5km of roadside tramway to Ormes was saved. Due to the outer terminus being alongside a fairly busy road, for reasons of passenger safety, the line was extended by a further 0.5km, with a deviation from the original route to Bellebat. Following 12 months of negotiations and restoration of the buildings and equipment, this short remnant of the once extensive system was re-opened on 23rd April 1966.

Although many of the TPT locomotives had already departed by the time of closure, the newly formed *Association du Musée des Transports de Pithiviers* (AMTP) was able to retain three of the TPT locomotives plus one of the Decauville 0-6-0Ts from the Toury refinery system. To supplement these survivors, a large number of characteristic locomotives from elsewhere have been acquired resulting in one of the most comprehensive collections of 60cm machines to be found in Europe. The station buildings have been restored to their original condition whilst the goods shed, which occupied much of the building, has been adapted as a museum. Here much of the locomotive fleet is displayed when not in use, the active

machines being confined to the adjoining shed and workshop complex.

The three TPT locomotives retained by the AMTP were the 1902 vintage Blanc-Misseron 0-6-0T (TPT 3-5), ALCO 2-6-2T (TPT 3-22) and Franco-Belge 0-8-0T (TPT 4-12). The Blanc-Misseron, which was the last locomotive to haul a train before closure, had the distinction of hauling the first train under the control of the AMTP along with the former Toury refinery Decauville *Type Progrès* 0-6-0T dating from 1928.

The additional locomotives which supplemented these survivors were a 1910 Couillet 0-6-0T from Maizy sugar refinery (subsequently transferred to the Chemin de Fer Touristique du Tarn), a diminutive Schneider 0-4-0T dating from 1870, two Decauville 0-4-0Ts built in 1905 and 1919, a 1938 La Meuse 2-6-0T also from Maizy, a Decauville *Type Royan* 0-6-2T built in 1902 and two of the ubiquitous "Feldbahn" 0-8-0Ts. These were built by Henschel and Hartmann, in 1917 and 1918 respectively. Another survivor from the TPT was the original Crochat petrol electric railcar dating from 1922. In addition a Gmeinder Type HF 130 of 1944 vintage used by the German occupying forces was acquired for shunting use.

The two former TPT locomotives that went to Meyzieu have subsequently been transferred to new homes following the closure of the Meyzieu line. The O & K Mallet is now to be found at the Chemin de Fer du Haut Rhône at Montalieu, east of Lyon, the successor to the Meyzieu line. After many years in store, the Franco-Belge 0-8-0T has recently been transferred to the CFT de la Vallée de l'Ouche at Bligny-sur-Ouche in central France. In addition the other two surviving ALCO 2-6-2Ts built in 1916 were saved for posterity, and are both very active locomotives at their respective homes. Former TPT 3-20 is to be found at the Froissy-Cappy-Dompierre line where it has been restored to its original condition. Meanwhile 3-23 came to the UK in 1967 and is now better known in much modified form as *Mountaineer* on the Ffestiniog Railway. To bring the ALCO story up to date, the AMTP based 3-22 following many years in store, has recently been the subject of a major overhaul to return this historic locomotive to traffic. As it has been restored to TPT condition, the three surviving ALCOs represent three distinct stages of their illustrious lives.

After languishing in a scrap dealers yard since 1965, the O & K 0-10-0T no. 5-3 has recently been rescued by the Froissy-Cappy-Dompierre organisation.

Following the end of passenger services in 1951, most of the coaches were scrapped and their frames used for additional freight wagons. Obviously a tourist railway required coaches in order to operate a service, so some action had to be taken. Three open sided "toast rack" vehicles, based on Royan KE type, and two semi-open similar to Calvados KG type, were constructed in the Pithiviers workshop during the early period of the AMTP operation. In 1966, four metre gauge end balcony coaches from the Tramway de Valenciennes were acquired. These were transferred to 60cm bogies from TPT goods stock and became an invaluable asset to the restored line. The only surviving TPT carriage was the 1942 built V6. Since 1951, this had been in a private collection in Paris, but in 1992 was repatriated to its original home. Following a thorough restoration, it re-entered service in 1994. The AMTP has also retained a number of TPT freight wagons, which see regular use on works trains and the occasional demonstration train.

In addition to the 60cm stock, the museum is also home to some important metre gauge exhibits. These include a Cail 2-6-0T built in 1895 for the CFD Charentes and a Blanc-Misseron saloon coach from the PO Corrèze dating from 1904. The latter was loaned for a short period in 1997 to the Chemin de Fer du Vivarais in order to operate with the former POC Mallet no.104 on its return to service.

Although not passing through spectacular scenery, a journey along this short railway is not without interest. Leaving the station, which is situated on the western edge of Pithiviers, the line passes the workshop and large engine shed. Descending a gradient of 1 in 45 the line turns left and passes under the SNCF line from Orléans to Malesherbes. Almost immediately two level crossings over minor roads are crossed plus another level crossing over a standard gauge siding leading to a fertiliser factory. The line now adopts its roadside position running alongside the D22 as far as Ormes. Initially the gradient is quite steep but soon levels out once the plateau is reached. Shortly before Ormes a recent addition to the landscape is passed. This is the new Pithiviers by pass, which crosses the railway and road on a lofty bridge.

At Ormes the line deviates to the left away from the original alignment to the terminus at Bellebat, 4km from Pithiviers. For many years Bellebat consisted of a run round loop and a van body serving as a shop. There was also a turning triangle literally buried in the undergrowth of the adjacent wood. During the 1990s major developments took place at the outer terminus. A replica of a typical French country station has been built which houses a shop and restaurant. In addition a large turning circle was constructed which enables a variety of permutations of locomotive operation. Some trains complete the entire round trip with the locomotive running smokebox first, followed by a bunker first trip up the line. However, on some occasions the locomotive runs around its train at Bellebat. With no turning facilities at Pithiviers, this flexible operating arrangement certainly presents the photographers with a wide choice of angles and views. Being a roadside line also allows many suitable vantage points.

Despite its short length, this surviving remnant of the original Tramway de Pithiviers à Toury is one of the most interesting preserved lines in France. The locomotive stock is probably the most comprehensive collection of 60cm machines in Europe, whilst the museum houses a large collection of narrow gauge photographs and artefacts. However, a word of warning for potential visitors: being a wholly volunteer organisation, the AMTP only operates on Sunday and Bank Holiday afternoons between May and October. In addition a restricted Saturday afternoon service runs during the high season. Despite this slight drawback, a visit is highly recommended to this historic line in Loiret. Pithiviers is approximately 100km south of Paris and 30km north of Orléans, at the intersection of the N152 and D921. The AMTP station is located at the western side of the town and clearly sign posted.

2.1.   The depot at Pithiviers was photographed on 2nd June 1962. O & K 0-4-4-0T Mallet no. 22-5 and Franco-Belge 0-8-0T no. 4-12 are seen with O & K 0-6-0T no. 3-6 just visible between them. (J.L.Rochaix / BVA).

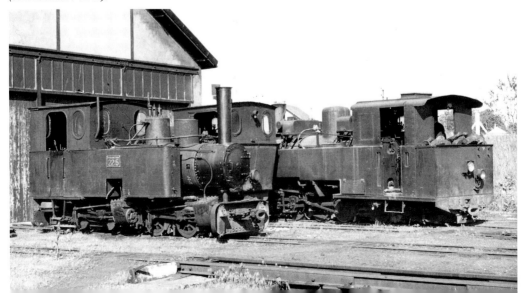

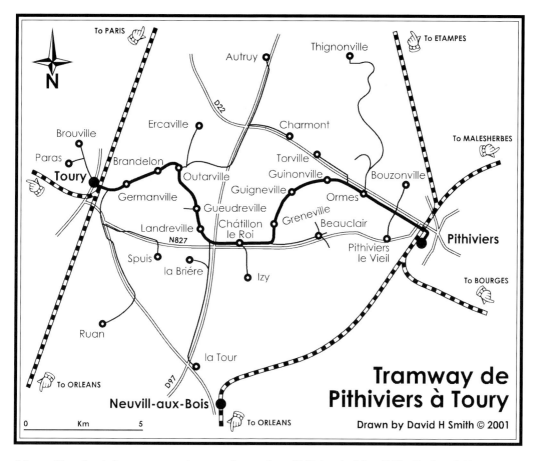

2.2.   Shunting is in progress at the extensive yards at Pithiviers in May 1963. Such activities were an everyday occurrence on the TPT during its heyday. (M.Grandguillaume / BVA).

2.3.   ALCO 2-6-2T no. 3-21 simmers with a short passenger train at Guigneville in December 1949. Of the four locomotives of this type acquired for use on the TPT in the 1930s, no. 3-21 is the only one not to have survived into preservation. (J.Chapuis / BVA).

2.4.   A short rake of wagons stand alongside a typical TPT station building at Greneville-en-Beauce on 2nd June 1962. (J.L.Rochaix / BVA).

2.5.   Franco-Belge 0-8-0T no. 4-13 shunts wagons at Outarville on 12th August 1961. The additional side tanks, fitted when the locomotive was converted from a tender/tank design, can clearly be seen in this view. (J.L.Rochaix / BVA).

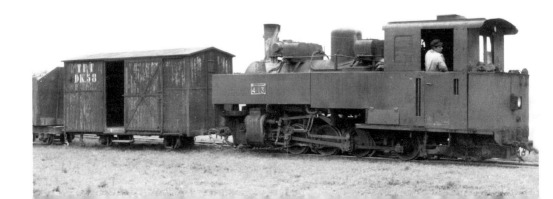

2.6.   Sister locomotive no.4-11 is seen hauling a load of beet wagons to the sugar refinery at Pithiviers on 2nd October 1959. The cradle supporting the front of the additional side tanks, which extend beyond the smokebox, is clearly visible. (D. Trevor Rowe).

2.7.   Another Franco-Belge 0-8-0T, no.4-10, shunts freight wagons at Toury in 1964. During the final decade of the TPT, these powerful locomotives handled most of the work on the railway. (J.Chapuis / BVA).

2.8.   One of the ubiquitous Decauville Type Progrès 0-6-0Ts is seen at Toury sugar refinery on 6th June 1962. The somewhat unkempt appearance of these locomotives during their later days of service is clearly shown. (J.L. Rochaix / BVA).

2.9.   Equally synonymous with the 60cm agricultural and industrial lines were the former WW 1 German "Feldbahn" 0-8-0Ts. Henschel no. 4-5 is seen at Pithiviers in December 1949.   (J.Chapuis / BVA).

2.10.   Blanc-Misseron 0-6-0T no. 3-5 rests at Châtillon-le-Roy on 2nd June 1962. This locomotive, built in 1902, was acquired second hand from the Tramway de Rotheneuf in 1926 and has been preserved by the AMTP at Pithiviers. (J.L.Rochaix /BVA).

2.11.   Orenstein and Koppel 0-4-4-0T Mallet no. 22-5 is seen at Pithiviers on 27th April 1963. This interesting locomotive has been preserved at Montalieu near Lyon. (D.Trevor Rowe).

2.12. Another product of O & K was this 0-10-0T no. 5-3, photographed in the locomotive shed at Pithiviers on 2nd October 1959. Basically an enlarged version of the standard "Feldbahn" design, this locomotive following many years in store has recently been rescued by the Froissy-Cappy-Dompierre organisation. (D.Trevor Rowe).

2.13. ALCO 2-6-2T no.3-22 is outside the depot at Pithiviers on 27th April 1963. This historic locomotive has recently been the subject of a major restoration project by the AMTP and is currently on display in the museum at Pithiviers. (D.Trevor Rowe).

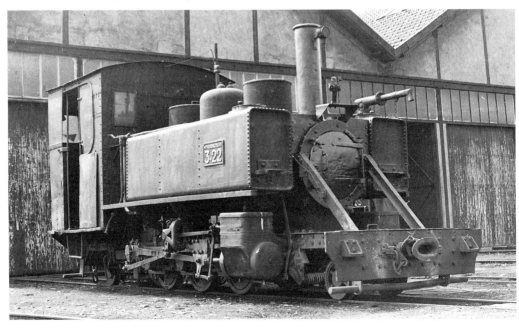

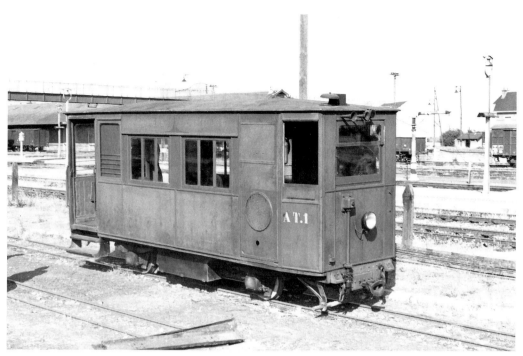

2.14.   *The original Crochat railcar of 1922 was photographed at Pithiviers in December 1949. This vehicle outlived its younger sisters and has been preserved by the AMTP. (J.Chapuis / BVA).*

2.15.   *Franco-Belge no.4-12 was photographed at Pithiviers on 25th May 1997.   The current AMTP operation, despite its short length, retains much of the character of the original TPT (D.Trevor Rowe).*

2.16.   La Meuse 2-6-0T no.9, formerly at Maizy, leaves Pithiviers with a British enthusiasts special on 29th May 1993. The rolling stock consists of the former Valenciennes coaches. (D.Trevor Rowe).

2.17.   Decauville Type Royan 0-6-2T no.10 begins the climb towards Ormes in August 1994. Note the passenger in the open wagon behind the locomotive receiving a shower of coal dust! The roadside position of the track bed is clearly seen in this view. (J.F. Organ).

2.18.   La Meuse no.9 arrives at the upper terminus at Bellebat with the British special on 29th May 1993. This was prior to the later developments, which transformed the site in 1995.   (D.Trevor Rowe).

2.19.   The diminutive Schneider 0-4-0T and La Meuse no.9 are seen on the old turning triangle at Bellebat, which was literally buried in the undergrowth. (D.Trevor Rowe).

2.20.   Franco-Belge no.4-12 departs from Bellebat and begins a circuit of the new turning circle in September 1996. The recreated station building can be seen behind the train. (J.F. Organ).

2.21.   Henschel 0-8-0T *"Feldbahn" no.4. shunts stock at Bellebat on July 22nd 2001. The van next to the locomotive is the mobile bar, which is attached to the first train of the day. (J.F. Organ).*

2.22.   *Back at Pithiviers, "Feldbahn" no.4 basks in the sunshine in the delightful surroundings alongside the museum on 22nd July 2001. (J.F. Organ).*

3. WORLD WAR 1 AND ITS LEGACY

Decauville's successful application of the 60cm gauge, portable railway systems, found an enthusiastic supporter in French military circles. As early as 1885, Colonel Péchot, a close friend of Paul Decauville, adapted the system to suit military needs. By 1888 the large fortified towns at Verdun, Toul, Epinal and Belfort had laid lines of "Systéme Péchot" 60cm track to connect the forts to the main citadels. To haul the gun carrying and ammunition trains, Péchot and Decauville had developed a double locomotive, based on Fairlie's successful design of articulated engines. Known as a Péchot-Bourdon, these 0-4-4-0T locomotives were built initially by Decauville using standard parts as much as possible. Later examples were built by the Baldwin Locomotive Works in the USA as part of a large military contract for the French Government.

When war was declared in 1914, it soon became obvious that this was to be far different to any previous conflict. Within a short time a line of trenches stretched from the Channel coast to the Swiss border with only a short area of "no mans land" between the opposing front lines. Behind the trenches, huge batteries of artillery were deployed whilst the battle remained in an almost constant position for three years, rarely moving more than a few yards in either direction. The French, having proved that their 60cm light railways were capable of moving enormous amounts of military equipment, both the British and German military leaders realised the need for similar systems behind their respective lines. So were born the War Department Light Railways (WDLR) of the British Army and the "Feldbahns" (Field Railways) developed by the German military. In due course, the American army became involved on the allied side, the USA locomotive builders, Baldwin and ALCO, having already supplied much equipment for the WDLR. These 60cm lines formed a link between the main line railway systems, well behind the front line, and the artillery batteries immediately behind the trenches. They conveyed ammunition, men and essential supplies in high capacity wagons of both bogie and four wheeled types.

One advantage of both sides employing the same gauge for their railways was of great benefit if the front line advanced in either direction. In such circumstances, ready built railways, and in many instances locomotives and rolling stock, were quickly taken over by the opposing forces. During the Somme campaign in 1916, some sections of railway "changed sides" on more than one occasion as the two armies advanced and retreated with regular monotony, gaining little ground in the process.

Locomotives at war

In addition to the Péchot-Bourdon double engines used by the French army, some of which were also used by the American troops, many locomotives of a more conventional design were supplied to the military of both the Allies and Germany. Such was the demand that many of the major locomotive builders of Great Britain, America and Germany supplied machines for the war effort.

The locomotives developed for use on these lightly laid systems were a sturdy breed, large numbers of which managed to survive the ravages of their wartime exploits. Hudswell Clarke supplied a number of their Class "G" 0-6-0WT design whilst Andrew Barclay provided a modified version of their "F" class 0-6-0WT. Ironically the latter machines were derived from a German design. However, these relatively small well tank locomotives were joined by many, much larger 13 Tonne 4-6-0T machines, built by Hunslet to a war office specification. The demand for locomotives was so great that the British works had difficulty in meeting demand. With the imminent arrival of American troops came a large consignment of 4-6-0Ts of similar size built by Baldwin, which became the most familiar sight on the military lines behind the allied lines. When the USA entered the war, they used a similar design built by both Baldwin and ALCO. These differed in being 2-6-2Ts and had the distinct advantage of being equally efficient when running in either direction, the 4-6-0Ts being prone to derailment when running bunker first. The locomotives built in Great Britain were of typical British design with plate frames, Belpaire boilers and Walschaerts valve gear. The American locomotives quite naturally bore all the hallmarks of their transatlantic design with bar frames, stove pipe chimneys, boiler top sand boxes and open backed cabs. In addition to the steam locomotives, petrol engine powered machines were also used. Most well known were the Simplex designs of the Motor Rail and Tramcar Co. Ltd, supplied in both 20hp and 40hp types. The latter were built in three variations, "open", "protected" or "armoured". Baldwin also produced large numbers of a 40hp 0-4-0 petrol mechanical locomotive, of more conventional appearance than the Simplex. Many of these were used by the French Army as well as the British and American troops.

The German "Feldbahn" systems used a standard design of 0-8-0T for the majority of their lines. These highly successful engines were built by many of the major German locomotive manufacturers. Borsig, Hartmann, Henschel, Humboldt, Krauss, Orenstein & Koppel and Schwartzkopff all supplied examples of these locomotives, which have become known as "Feldbahns" throughout the world. The majority were the standard 0-8-0T design whilst some had a tender and shorter side tanks, thus becoming 0-8-0TTs. As mentioned in the previous chapter, there were also some "stretched" versions built as 0-10-0Ts. Like the Allies, the German military also employed internal combustion machines in some of the more sensitive areas. Their standard engine was a Deutz 10hp single cylinder unit, built in large numbers despite their obvious deficiency in power output.

The Legacy of War

Following the Armistice in 1918, Northern France was battered and torn following four years of war. Although much of the equipment from the military railways was returned to their native soil at the end of hostilities, many locomotives and much rolling stock remained in France and were destined to see many more years service in far less frenzied circumstances. The metre gauge lines that had become involved in the conflict, particularly those in the Verdun area, had borrowed locomotives from elsewhere in France. The majority of these were quickly returned to their original homes. However, the situation with the 60cm equipment was rather different. The locomotives were either repatriated to their home countries or remained in France. The latter were acquired by dealers and subsequently sold to a large variety of new homes throughout the country.

As noted in the previous chapter, the sugar beet area in Loiret had a large network of 60cm lines supplying the refineries at Pithiviers and Toury. However, the major sugar beet producing area was to the west of Reims where many refineries had their independent railway systems. The principal 60cm lines were at Maizy, Coucy le

Château and Cramaille together with the metre gauge systems at Neuilly St Front and Nangis. The 60cm lines had initially been operated with the ubiquitous Decauville and Couillet 0-4-0T and 0-6-0T locomotives, hauling open wagons from the same sources. By the end of hostilities many of these overworked machines were in need of replacement. With a surplus of locomotives from the military field railways available, many of them in excellent condition, ready buyers were soon found for some of these redundant machines. The most popular choice was the 10 Tonne German 0-8-0T "Feldbahn" type, large numbers of which were available. These excellent, powerful locomotives, were soon to be seen at work at all the major sugar beet refinery systems.

The largest, and longest lived of these lines in Aisne, was the Sucrerie de Maizy which survived until 1964. With a total mileage of 80km, this was a most impressive system. Traversing flat and windswept country, much of it laid alongside minor roads, it was a typical example of these agricultural lines that supplied the large sugar refineries. During the 1960s, improved roads and cheaper transport by lorry brought about their downfall and subsequent closure. However, during their heyday, steam reigned supreme at Maizy. In 1938, the large fleet of "Feldbahn" 0-8-0Ts and smaller French built machines had to be supplemented. The result was the arrival of two large and impressive 2-6-0Ts built by La Meuse at Liege in Belgium. These 13 Tonne engines, nos. 8 and 9 in the Maizy list were at the time the largest locomotives operating on the 60cm lines. Fortunately both have survived into preservation, no.8 at Montalieu and no.9 at Pithiviers.

As recorded in the previous chapter, in 1945 some powerful Franco-Belge 0-8-0Ts became available, four being acquired by the TPT. These 19 Tonne monsters became the pinnacle of locomotive development on the French 60cm systems. In addition to the TPT locomotives, two more went to the Sucreries Ternyck, Coucy le Château to join their fleet of "Feldbahns". When the Coucy line closed in 1962, the two Franco-Belge locomotives were transferred to Pithiviers, being used as a source of spare parts for their hard working sisters.

Although the wartime military supply lines were removed shortly after the end of hostilities, as will be recorded in the next chapter, one at least did survive and was adapted for commercial use. This line still operates as a tourist line, providing a lasting reminder of the part played by the narrow gauge railway systems during one of Europe's darkest periods.

The Tourist Lines

The next chapter concentrates on one former WW 1 railway, which has survived into the preservation era. However, throughout France, numerous tourist lines have evolved during the last 40 years, many of them on completely new locations or on former standard gauge track beds. Invariably these lines use locomotives and equipment from the wartime military lines, at least one "Feldbahn" 0-8-0T has become an almost indispensable item at the majority of them! Although found throughout the country, two important examples of these ventures are to be found in the outer suburbs of Paris.

Chemin de Fer de Saint-Eutrope

Situated at Évry, a new town on the southern outskirts of Paris, is a country park near the Hippodrome des Arcades racecourse. As part of a proposal to increase leisure activities in the park, a narrow gauge railway was considered to be a worthwhile attraction. Consequently a collection of locomotives and rolling stock owned by M.Guillemont formed the nucleus of the railway, which was built by a team of local enthusiasts. Construction began in 1975 and was completed in time for the opening in 1978. The 2.5km track consists of two balloon loops, which are connected by a long straight central section, runs through pleasant woodland and open fields. At the eastern loop, near the site entrance and car park, a large depot and station was constructed. As Évry is situated close to the Decauville works at Corbeil, it is no surprise that a museum dedicated to the Decauville company is being created alongside the railway.

The locomotive fleet consists of three 0-8-0T "Feldbahns" including two built by Henschel and one by Krauss. Decauville are represented by three 0-6-0T *Type Progrès* machines built between 1916 and 1920. The collection is completed by a Jung 0-4-0WT dating from 1918, and a Couillet 0-6-0T built in 1910. In addition, internal combustion powered locomotives are also present. These include a Deutz loco-tractor from WW 1 and larger machines built by Gmeinder and Billard. Rolling stock consists of a varied selection of passenger and freight wagons, including two carriages from the Neufchatel tramway. For the more hardy passengers, open bogie coaches based on WW 1 wagon frames are also available.

The Chemin de Fer de Saint-Eutrope normally operates on Saturday, Sunday and Bank Holiday afternoons between Easter and November. Évry is located near the RN 7 approximately half way between Paris and Fontainebleau.

Chemin de Fer des Chanteraines

To the north west of Paris, near Gennevilliers, another leisure park was created during the 1970s close to the Ile St.Denis in the River Seine. Built in stages between 1984 and 1991, the line totals 5.5km in length following a sinuous course including a spiral loop. From the terminal station close to the Pont d'Epinay, which crosses the twin branches of the Seine, the line initially follows the south bank of the river for 1.3km before curving acutely to the right into the park. The route then climbs abruptly to cross the main road through the park on a long steel viaduct before descending over the aforementioned spiral loop. After the spiral the line runs close to the lake before crossing the A 86 Autoroute by a long concrete bridge. Finally the track swings round to the right to enter the far terminus and depot at Gennevilliers.

The locomotive stock is an exception to the rule in that it does not include a "Feldbahn" in the collection. However it does have two of the ubiquitous Decauville products, a 1919 vintage 0-6-0T and a 0-4-0T built under license by Borsig in 1911. The German connection is completed by an Orenstein & Koppel 0-4-0WT, dating from 1905. The Diesel fleet comprises of four 120 hp Plymouth machines, a Campagne 40 hp tractor built in 1928 and two Socofer 60 hp units with hydraulic transmission, dating from 1981. Rolling stock is mainly open sided vehicles including six 40 seat examples built by Socofer.

In 1994 to celebrate its 20th anniversary, the Chanteraines line was graced with a visit by the George England 0-4-0ST *Palmerston* from the Ffestiniog Railway. As a return gesture, the two Decauvilles paid a visit to Porthmadog in 1995 for the FR Gala, along with two other visiting locomotives from France.

The Chemin de Fer des Chanteraines usually operates between March and November on Saturday, Sunday, Bank Holiday and Wednesday afternoons. The park is situated off the RN 186 near Villeneuve-la-Garenne, the entrance being on the Boulevard Charles de Gaulle.

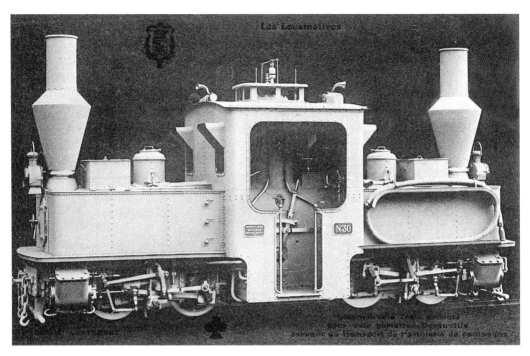

3.1.   Works photograph of a Péchot-Bourdon 0-4-4-0T. These locomotives, closely based on the Fairlie design, were largely constructed from standard Decauville parts. (Coll.   J.K.Williams).

3.2.   A "Feldbahn" 0-8-0T is transhipped onto 60cm tracks behind the German front line during World War 1. (Coll.   R.N.Redman).

3.3. *"Fruits of War". Captured "Feldbahn" 0-8-0Ts are lined up at the central repair depot of the WDLR at Beaurainville during the latter months of WW 1. (Coll. R.N.Redman).*

3.4. *A War Department Light Railway marshalling yard, "somewhere in France". A number of Baldwin 4-6-0T locomotives can be seen in the distance, along with a variety of rolling stock. (Coll. K.Taylorson / Lens of Sutton).*

3.5. *Canadian troops labour at an ammunition loading point in February 1918. Note the numerous horses in the distance, still being used despite the increasing mechanisation of the war at this late stage. (Coll. K.Taylorson / IWM).*

3.6.   *German troops travel through woodland near Braquis in April 1917. The motive power is a Deutz 10hp Loco-Tractor. (Coll.   K.Taylorson).*

3.7.   *Couillet 0-6-0T no.1 is raising steam at Maizy Sugar Refinery on 10th November 1962. (D. Trevor Rowe).*

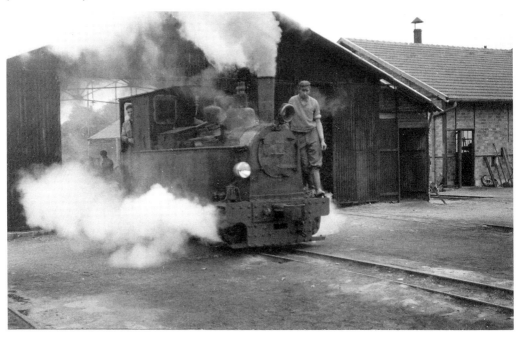

3.8. Another view of Couillet no.1 at Maizy is from 10th November 1962. This locomotive, built in 1910, is now preserved at the Chemin de Fer Touristique du Tarn as recorded in **Southern France Narrow Gauge**. (D.Trevor Rowe).

3.9. Krauss "Feldbahn" 0-8-0T no.5 is seen at the coal stage at Maizy on the same date. Note the large stock of briquettes alongside the locomotive. (D.Trevor Rowe).

3.10.   La Meuse 2-6-0Ts are at work in the sugar beet fields at Maizy. No.8 departs with a loaded train of beet whilst no.9 waits in a siding on 10ᵗʰ November 1962. (D.Trevor Rowe).

3.11.   Another view of a La Meuse features no.8 as it departs en route to the refinery. Both of the former Maizy La Meuse 2-6-0Ts are currently at Pithiviers. No.8 is undergoing an extensive overhaul on behalf of its owners at Montalieu, whilst no.9 is in regular service on the AMTP. (D.Trevor Rowe).

3.12.   The locomotive depot at the Chemin de Fer de Saint-Eutrope at Évry. A Coillet 0-6-0T and a Henschel 0-8-0T "Feldbahn" are seen, with a Decauville 0-6-0T just visible in the background. This scene was recorded on 28ᵗʰ May 1994. (D.Trevor Rowe).

3.13.   Jung 0-4-0WT heads a fully laden passenger train at Saint-Eutrope on 28th May 1994. The open sided bogie coaches are built on former WW 1 wagon frames. (D. Trevor Rowe).

3.14.   Henschel 0-8-0T "Feldbahn" no.1535 is seen superbly restored at Saint-Eutrope, on 12th August 1995. With so many of these former German military locomotives in preservation, they certainly are a "Legacy of War". (D. Trevor Rowe).

3.15.   Decauville 0-6-0T **Type Progrès** *no.770, dating from 1919, is at work on the Chemin de Fer des Chanteraines on 26th May 1997. This locomotive paid a visit to the Ffestiniog Railway in 1995, along with a Borsig 0-4-0T from the same stable. (D.Trevor Rowe).*

3.16.   Another view of Decauville no.770, shows it at Chanteraines on the same occasion. The immaculate state of the stock and infrastructure of this small railway are evident in this photograph. (D.Trevor Rowe).

4. FROISSY-CAPPY-DOMPIERRE

In 1915, during the height of World War I, the French army constructed a 60cm military supply line alongside the southern side of the Somme canal between Froissy, Cappy and Peronne. The Somme canal was constructed during the 19th Century adjacent to the River Somme in order to provide a navigable route to the channel coast. A wharf was situated at Cappy Port, a short distance from the village of the same name. In 1916 the Allies launched a major offensive in Picardy with the front line a short distance to the east of Cappy village. The ensuing Battle of the Somme was destined to become one of the longest and bloodiest periods of the conflict. The fighting raged in the area between 1916 and 1918 whilst the French and British forces opposed the German army which held the Santerre Plateau and Dompierre village. The railway alongside the canal was well screened in the wooded valley and served the allied forces with supplies. During the battle, the Froissy to Cappy section was regularly carrying over 1500 tonnes of ammunition and equipment daily, which equated to about 200 wagon loads.

The line ran from Froissy, where it connected with the metre gauge route from Albert to Montdidier, to Peronne near the front line. After the Armistice in 1918, the railway was utilised to assist in clearing the debris of war and transporting food and materials for rebuilding the severely damaged villages. To facilitate this work, additional 60cm tracks were laid in the area around Peronne whilst a deviation from the original formation at Cappy ran up a steep climb to the plateau and Dompierre.

The reconstruction work lasted until 1924, during which period local quarries, brickworks and notably the sugar refinery at Dompierre had utilised the railway for their needs. Ultimately the latter concern took over operation of the line from the département in conjunction with the quarry at Cappy. In order to improve the operation of the railway to suit their purposes, the new operators built a new route to the plateau in 1927, using heavier rail than hitherto. This deviated from the original formation at Cappy Port and immediately entered a 300 metre long tunnel, which bypassed Cappy village. From the tunnel, the line climbed through the woods on a less severe gradient via a double reversal (zig-zag) before rejoining the old route on the Santerre Plateau. An extension to Chaulnes was laid in 1931 to provide a link with the main line system. In this form the line survived, virtually unknown outside the immediate locality. The quarry delivered stone to the canal wharf whilst the refinery transported wagons of sugar in sacks or molasses in tank wagons to Cappy. On the return journey coal and other equipment was delivered to the refinery. During WW 2, a train of molasses was attacked by a British aircraft, which no doubt assumed it was carrying materials of importance for the occupying forces! During the period of occupation, the German troops must have felt quite at home with the five "Feldbahn" locomotives that had operated the line since 1927. By 1954, the extensions to Peronne and Chaulnes had been removed, leaving the line from Cappy to Dompierre as the last remnant of this once extensive system.

In 1942, the steam locomotives were joined by two 100 hp Coferna diesel locomotives which had to have their cabs reduced in height to pass through the tunnel. The last steam locomotives were retired in 1946, being replaced by three Plymouth loco-tractors. For the next two decades the line continued to transport sugar to the waiting barges at Cappy Port. These could carry 250 tonnes whilst a train of three 10 tonne wagons could, with some overloading, just about manage 40 tonnes. Eight empty wagons could be hauled up the grade, the number limited by the length of the reversing stubs on the "zig-zag". With an increase in road traffic and improved roads, it was obvious that this arrangement was somewhat uneconomic. Operation of the line ceased in 1972, whilst the refinery closed in 1988 having used road haulage during its final years.

Le Chemin de Fer Touristique Froissy-Cappy-Dompierre

In 1970 an organisation known as *"L'Association Picarde pour la Preservation et L'Entretien des Vehicules Anciens* (APPEVA) was formed with the intention of finding a suitable length of track on which to set up a working 60cm museum line. The situation at Froissy was ideal for their purposes, being situated mid-way between Paris and Lille and within easy reach of Amiens. The Somme valley with its river and canal was a popular destination for fishing and visitors wishing to escape from the rigours of city life.

Initially, only the canal side section between Froissy and Cappy Port was available to the new society, which in June 1971 operated its first train along 1 km of track. The first train was hauled by a 70 hp Billard loco-tractor whilst the first steam hauled train ran on 31st July of that year. This was headed by a small Neumeyer 0-4-0T, the passenger stock consisting of some open sided coaches constructed on the frames of old US Army wagons. By October 1971, 5000 passengers had been carried and with the anticipated increase in traffic, more rolling stock would be required. 1972 saw the arrival of more steam locomotives, many requiring extensive overhaul before they could enter service, whilst the primitive locomotive depot at Froissy was supplemented by a wooden carriage shed. Passenger numbers rose to 13000 and yet more rolling stock was added with some rather more comfortable fully enclosed coaches to supplement the open sided stock.

In 1974, APPEVA were able to take over the whole line, initially working over 3.5km to the top of the "zig-zag". The final section to Dompierre was reopened in 1976 following improvements to the permanent way and level crossing on the Santerre Plateau. Since then the Chemin de Fer Touristique Froissy-Cappy-Dompierre (CFCD) has continued to expand with some superb locomotive restorations to its credit. In 1996, to celebrate the 25th anniversary of APPVA, a magnificent new museum and restaurant complex was opened at Froissy. Adjoining the museum a new locomotive depot was constructed in the form of a semi-roundhouse connected to a turntable. The original depot and carriage shed nearby remain in use as the engineering base for the railway. At the same time, the CFCD name was changed to a new title of *Le petit train de la Haute Somme et son Musée des C.F. Militaires and Industriels.* However, it is still more normally referred to by its original name, which links the locations served by the line, and avoids confusion with the metre gauge Baie de Somme line on the channel coast.

A journey along the line normally begins from the island platform at the small terminal station at Froissy. This is situated alongside the road bridge over the canal, near the route of the aforementioned metre gauge line that closed in 1954. From Froissy the line drops down a gradient to the canal towpath with which it then proceeds to run parallel. Within a short distance, the new museum and depot complex is reached where there is also a station platform. In conjunction with the new development, a large car park has also been provided. As a result, this will in future become the principal departure point for journeys along the line, the car parking facilities at the original Froissy terminus being far too restricted.

From the museum, the line continues to follow the towpath, partly screened from the canal by a row of trees. On the other side of the track a wooded cliff rises abruptly whilst some sidings, used for storage of rolling stock awaiting restoration, are almost buried beneath the trees at the base of the cliff face. Within a short distance, Cappy Port is reached where a passing loop is situated. On normal working days, when one of the smaller steam locomotives is in use, a change of motive power takes place at this location. For the steep climb though the tunnel and "zig-zag", one of the more powerful diesel locomotives takes over for the remaining 5km to Dompierre.

Departing from Cappy Port, the line plunges into the 300 metre curved tunnel which passes behind the village. At the exit of the tunnel, the line almost immediately crosses a level crossing over a minor road before climbing into the wooded slopes of the valley. Within a short time, the train stops in a headshunt, after which the locomotive propels its coaches in reverse along the intermediate incline of the "zig-zag". This terminates in another headshunt after which the locomotive continues to haul the train up the remainder of the climb. Emerging from the trees, the line reaches the plateau and crosses the D164, which it then runs alongside until the upper terminus on the outskirts of Dompierre is reached. Originally the line crossed the road again at this point, terminating at the sugar refinery. Since the closure of the refinery, this short final section has been abandoned thereby eliminating the level crossing at this point. The current terminus is surrounded by fields of various arable crops, situated near the Dompierre football ground.

Following a short stop whilst the locomotive runs round the train, the return journey commences along the Santerre Plateau. Once again, locomotives are changed at Cappy-Port, unless one of the larger steam locomotives is in use, in which case it will complete the entire route. During the return journey, a long stop will be made at the museum to enable passengers to view the excellent exhibits. These include locomotives, rolling stock and other railway artefacts associated with the 60cm gauge systems of both military and industrial background.

The locomotive collection is very comprehensive from a wide variety of sources. From the original industrial line of 1927, the only surviving machines are the two Coferna diesel locomotives and one of the Plymouth loco-tractors.

The Coferna machines were built in 1941 by *Société de Constructions Ferroviaires et Navales* at Sables d'Olonne in Vendée. They were originally fitted with 100hp two-stroke CLM diesel engines

Since their acquisition by APPEVA, the original power units have been replaced by more powerful diesel engines. T24 is now fitted with a 212hp Tatra air-cooled unit whilst T25 is now powered by a more conventional 180hp Iveco water-cooled engine. The 1946 Plymouth loco-tractor, which spent most of its working life shunting at the sugar refinery, is used for lighter duties.

As mentioned above, the first steam locomotive to arrive in 1971 was a small 0-4-0T, built by Neumeyer of Munich in 1922. This, typically German industrial locomotive, was soon joined by many from a variety of sources. Two of the ubiquitous Decauville *Type Progrès* 0-6-0T machines built in 1916 and 1928 were joined by three of the equally ubiquitous "Feldbahn" 0-8-0T locomotives, similar to those that worked on the line prior to 1946. These were built by Henschel in 1917, Krauss and Borsig in 1918. The Borsig locomotive, which formerly worked on a forestry line in Poland, differs from the others in being a 0-8-0TT. This version has a tender and smaller side tanks.

To represent the allied contribution to World War 1, an ALCO 2-6-2T from Pithiviers was acquired in 1980. Formerly TPT no. 3-20, this locomotive has been beautifully restored to its WW 1 condition and carries its WDLR livery of green ochre with WD insignia. In 1995, it appeared at the Ffestiniog Railway Gala when it worked alongside its former sister 3-23, now better known as *Mountaineer* on the F.R. In 1996, the latter paid a visit to the CFCD, along with other visiting locomotives from Britain and Germany, for the 25th anniversary celebrations.

Another smaller locomotive is a 0-4-0T built by Henschel in 1937. This machine was acquired in 1979 and bears the name *Floralie*, having worked at a line constructed in 1967 to serve a large floral exhibition at Orléans. The less powerful locomotives are used during the quieter periods of operation and are confined to the canal side section between Froissy and Cappy Port. The "Feldbahns" and ALCO are permitted to venture through the tunnel and "zig-zag" along with the two most powerful machines in the collection. These are both 0-8-0s, products of Vulcan and Franco-Belge. The Vulcan was built in 1925 at Stettin for the Mecklenburg-Pommersche Bahn in the former East Germany. Following closure of that line in 1970, this large machine no. 99-3461 spent eight years in Britain, having been acquired by a group intending to take over the Vale of Rheidol line from British Rail. Having spent much of that period in store at New Romney, the locomotive was transferred to Froissy in 1978 following the failure of the Rheidol scheme. The most powerful machine working on the CFCD is the 1944 Franco-Belge Type KDL 0-8-0TT.

This is one of the locomotives that worked at the sugar refinery at Coucy le Château until 1962, and transferred to Pithiviers following the closure of the Coucy line. This impressive locomotive has been rebuilt in its original form as a tender-tank locomotive. Having the tender attached has allowed the additional side tanks to be removed, resulting in a far more pleasing appearance. As mentioned in chapter 2, the former TPT O & K 0-10-0T has recently been rescued and is currently displayed in the museum in a very rusty condition. Funds are being raised to restore this important exhibit to working condition.

In addition to the Coferna and Plymouth engines already mentioned, a number of internal combustion powered machines have been added to the collection since 1971. Following the arrival in that year of the 70hp Billard tractor, machines associated with the military past history of the line have been acquired. Two Simplexes of 20hp and 40hp represent the British contribution whilst the USA is represented by two 40hp Baldwin loco-tractors. Smaller French traction include a Socofer tractor built in 1968 and a small draisine (track inspection car) built by Speeder.

Rolling stock comprises of mainly "home produced" passenger stock built on the frames of former goods wagons, some of which date back to WW 1. As mentioned previously, these are mainly open sided vehicles, with curtains to protect passengers in inclement weather. In addition some rather more salubrious rolling stock has been built with doors and windows for protection. The goods vehicles are mainly bogie wagons of both closed and open types, many dating from the military era plus later examples from the industrial period.

As in the case of the AMTP, the Froissy-Cappy-Dompierre line is a voluntary run operation, which naturally affects the number of operating days. These are usually restricted to Sundays and Bank Holiday afternoons between May and September. Additional services are normally provided on Wednesdays and Saturdays between July and early September plus Thursdays during August. A visit to the CFCD is highly recommended, with its interesting combination of military and industrial heritage. Froissy is approximately 25km east of Amiens, near Bray-sur-Somme and Albert.

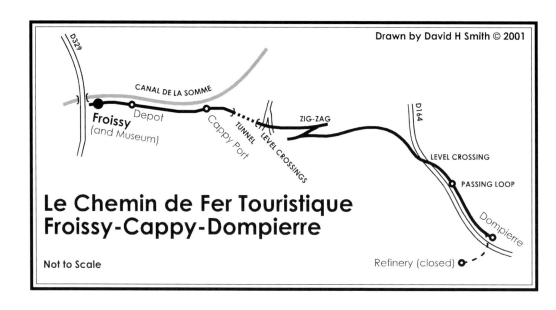

Drawn by David H Smith © 2001

CANAL DE LA SOMME

D329

Froissy
(and Museum)

Depot

Cappy Port

TUNNEL

LEVEL CROSSINGS

ZIG-ZAG

D164

LEVEL CROSSING

PASSING LOOP

Dompierre

Le Chemin de Fer Touristique
Froissy-Cappy-Dompierre

Not to Scale

Refinery (closed) ⭘ ⁻ ⁻

4.1 Franco-Belge 0-8-0TT no.10 waits outside the museum at Froissy, on the CFCD. Compare the appearance of this locomotive, restored to its original condition, with the 0-8-0T variants at Pithiviers. This photograph shows this impressive machine shortly after its return to service in 1998. (D.H. Smith).

4.2.   A busy scene at the Froissy locomotive depot was recorded in September 1998. ALCO no.9, Krauss "Feldbahn" no.4 and Franco-Belge no.10 are seen in this view, with Borsig 0-8-0TT just visible behind the ALCO. (D.H. Smith)

4.3.   The light and airy museum at Froissy, which contains a large collection of former WW 1 and industrial locomotives and rolling stock. (D.Trevor Rowe).

4.4. **Mountaineer,** *on a visit from the Ffestiniog Railway on 18th May 1996, passes the depot at Froissy with a train bound for Dompierre. The driver is David Black, assistant works manager at Boston Lodge Engineering.* **(D.Trevor Rowe).**

4.5. **Krauss 0-8-0T "Feldbahn" no.4.** *approaches Cappy-Port with a short freight train from Froissy in September 1998.* **(D.H. Smith).**

4.6. Franco-Belge 0-8-0TT no.10 passes ALCO 2-6-2T no. 9 (formerly TPT 3-20) at Cappy-Port on 27th September 1998. The rolling stock has mainly been built at Froissy on the frames of former freight wagons, many dating from WW 1. (D.H. Smith).

4.7. On July 14th 2001, Borsig 0-8-0TT no.7 arrives at Cappy-Port. In deference to the French National Holiday, the German locomotive is bedecked with "the Tricolore". (J.F. Organ).

4.8.   *The Borsig 0-8-0TT hands over to Coferna diesel locomotive no.T24 for the remainder of the journey to Dompierre. The Borsig locomotive is a tender version of the standard "Feldbahn" design. (J.F. Organ).*

4.9.   *ALCO 2-6-2T no.9 "bursts" from the tunnel and immediately crosses the ungated level crossing on the climb from Cappy-Port to the Santerre Plateau on 27th September 1998. Only the more powerful steam locomotives are permitted to haul trains on this section of the Froissy-Cappy-Dompierre line. (D.H. Smith).*

4.10.   During its visit to the CFCD in 1996, Mountaineer attacks the third level of the "zig-zag" between Cappy and Dompierre. Regular Ffestiniog driver Paul Ingham is in charge on this occasion. (D.Trevor Rowe).

4.11.   Vulcan 0-8-0TT no.8 approaches the summit of the climb to the Santerre Plateau on 19th May 1996. This locomotive spent a number of years stored at New Romney, being one of two similar machines acquired in 1970 as part of an abortive scheme to take over the Vale of Rheidol Railway from British Rail. (D.Trevor Rowe).

4.12.   *The Franco-Belge 0-8-0TT stands at a passing loop on the Santerre Plateau. Note the close proximity of the crops to the railway, so typical of the rural narrow gauge lines of France.   (D.H. Smith).*

4.13.   *ALCO 2-6-2T no.9 waits at Dompierre on 30ᵗʰ May 1993. This former TPT locomotive has been superbly restored to its original WW 1 condition. (D.Trevor Rowe).*

4.14.   *Coferna diesel locomotive no. T25 arrives at Dompierre with a freight train in 1998. This machine has had its original 100 hp CLM engine replaced by a 180 hp Iveco unit, necessitating the increased height of the bonnet and radiator. (D.H. Smith).*

5. THE GERMAN CONNECTION IN ALSACE

Following the Franco-Prussian war of 1870-71, much of North Eastern France in Alsace and Lorraine was transferred to German authority. This had a lasting effect, which remains to this day with cultural and architectural features showing a definite Germanic influence. The area reverted to French control following the Armistice in 1918.

As in many aspects of everyday life in the sequestrated provinces, railway development also followed German practices, particularly with the narrow gauge lines. Although the German systems normally favoured 75cm, their military lines at that time used the less common gauge of 70cm. This was subsequently changed before WW 1 to 60cm to the lasting benefit of many French systems. One line that was built to the 70cm gauge was constructed in 1884 for the specific purpose of transporting timber from the forests of the Vosges hills, between Strasbourg and Sarrebourg.

The Forest of Abreschviller covers an area of more than 7,000 hectares on hillsides reaching over 1000 metres in altitude. Planted mainly with fir and beech trees, exploitation of the forests was proving difficult to accomplish. A complex system of lines throughout the forests was constructed which at their greatest extent totalled 73km, plus an additional 25km of temporary tracks laid to the felling areas. Its sole purpose was to transport lumberjacks to the felling areas and return with timber for the sawmills. In conjunction with the forestry railway system, a standard gauge branch from Sarrebourg to Abreschviller was opened in 1892 to facilitate the transport of cut timber to their final destinations. Two violent storms in 1892 and 1902 which brought down vast numbers of trees provided added incentive to develop the operation, which during its heyday was handling some 40,000 cubic metres of timber annually.

The rolling stock used for transporting the timber usually consisted of four-wheel bolster trucks. These were connected to each other, and the locomotive, by long coupling poles due to the length of the almost complete tree trunks transported to the sawmills. As many as five pairs of trucks could sometimes be marshalled into a train as it wound its way around the sinuous curves through the forests. As is often the case in such operations, the loaded trains were running downhill which placed the emphasis on braking rather than power output of the locomotives. For transporting lumberjacks and other equipment into the forests, some open bogie wagons were utilised, protection from the elements being considered unnecessary! However, as some concession, tarpaulin sheets fitted over hoop frames were sometimes added to these vehicles.

During the 1960s the railway was considered to be life expired, whilst advances in specialist road transport had further produced economies that could not be overlooked. In 1966, the majority of the system had been dismantled, apart from the 6km section from Abreschviller to Grand-Soldat.

Chemin de Fer D'Abreschviller

The scenic attractions of the area had long been appreciated, to the extent that many special passenger trains had been operated during the years shortly before the line closed in 1966. As a direct result, the potential for a tourist railway was clearly seen. With the co-operation of the forestry service, the département authorities and FACS, the retention of the final 6km of line was successfully achieved. Following the overhaul of the remaining locomotives and rolling stock, much track relaying and the acquisition of suitable passenger carrying vehicles, the first train under the new administration ran on 1st June 1968.

The preserved section of the system is what could be described as the "main line" of the original network. From this main artery, numerous branch lines climbed into the forests via a complex series of junctions. Many of these routes have been converted into forest walks, although many have been adopted for road transport serving the still active forestry industry.

A journey along the surviving 6km begins at the small station at Abreschviller, situated near the depot and sawmills. Nearby is the now closed SNCF station, at the end of the former freight only 15km branch from Sarrebourg. Leaving the station, the line runs below the town of Abreschviller and crosses some minor roads on the level. The route then begins to run parallel to a minor road and the River Sarre Rouge, which is mainly screened by trees. This section is notable for some very tight curvature. Ultimately the intermediate station at Romelstein is reached after which the line crosses the river and a road. The final section of the route climbs steeply to the upper terminus at Grand-Soldat, running alongside the road in traditional tramway fashion, before passing through the centre of the small hamlet. The steep climb continues to the upper terminus where a new station has been built alongside a former saw mill which has been converted into a museum devoted to the railway and forestry industry.

Following the closure of the forestry system in 1966, the remaining locomotives and rolling stock were inherited by the replacement tourist operation. These included two steam locomotives and a diesel powered machine, which have hauled the majority of services since 1968. The oldest and most powerful locomotive is a 0-4-4-0T Mallet built in Germany by Heilbronn in 1906. This Fifteen Tonne compound machine is a typical example of the type of locomotive used on the system in its heyday. The other steam locomotive inherited in 1966 is a Decauville 0-6-0T *Type Progrès* of 1928 vintage, a rare example of this design adapted to the 70cm gauge. The diesel locomotive is a 1953-built Coferna fitted with a 100hp Willeme engine and Voith hydraulic transmission. Also acquired by the new regime were two inspection vehicles constructed in 1925 and 1930 from Renault and Hotchkiss motor vehicles.

Since 1966, extra motive power and rolling stock have been added, the latter being of prior importance as the original line obviously had no passenger coaches. The steam locomotive fleet has been bolstered by the addition of a Jung 0-6-0TT, built in 1944 for the 75cm German military railways. Another machine of German military origin is one of the small Deutz loco-tractors from the WW 1 60cm lines. The passenger carrying stock has been acquired from a variety of sources throughout Europe. Two open-sided coaches from the 60cm floral exhibition line at Orléans were among the first arrivals, whilst from Germany were two 36 seat Diebold coaches and four 40 seat vehicles built in Schirmeck for a military railway at Donon. Finally, from Switzerland there arrived four splendid coaches built in 1930 by Neuhausen for the 80cm Wengernalp Bahn. Various items of rolling stock from the forestry system have survived including bolster timber trucks, bogie wagons and two closed vans. One of the latter has been converted into a mobile ticket office.

Situated 45km west of Strasbourg and 15km south of Sarrebourg in the Vosges hills of Alsace, the Chemin de Fer D'Abreschviller is one of the most unique of the tourist lines of Northern France. The railway generally operates at weekends and bank holidays between May and October with a daily service during July and August. Despite its short length, it has much to offer in respect of its scenic attractions and equipment. With over 35,000 passenger journeys annually, the future of this delightful railway is very secure and is one of the major tourist attractions of the area.

5.1.   Shortly before the Abreschviller Forest Railway ceased operation in 1966, FACS organised a special excursion over part of the system. On 12th June 1966, the Heilbronn 0-4-4-0T Mallet is preparing to leave Abreschviller whilst the passengers board the bogie wagons formerly used by lumberjacks. (D.Trevor Rowe).

Cormeilles-en-Parisis

Although the 70cm gauge was normally confined to the former German controlled areas of France, an exception was an industrial line situated to the north west of Paris. This was an extensive system owned by the gypsum works of Lambert Frères at Cormeilles-en-Parisis, operated by a fleet of twelve locomotives. These were invariably German built locomotives, although at least one originated from Czechoslovakia, built by CKD in 1940. They were all 0-4-0T well tank or side tank locomotives, the German machines being built by either Orenstein & Koppel or Henschel between 1912 and 1925. The CKD locomotive was almost purchased by the Talyllyn Railway in 1974, the sale unfortunately falling through at the last minute.

The reason for the railway system was twofold. The hopper trucks carried gypsum from the works to high level sidings, where the contents were discharged into standard gauge wagons below. Secondly, a 3km line ran to a wharf on the River Seine where the gypsum was transferred to barges for onward delivery. Sadly, the fascinating Cormeilles line, one of the most intensively used industrial railways in France, closed in the late 1960s, another victim of the increased use of road transport.

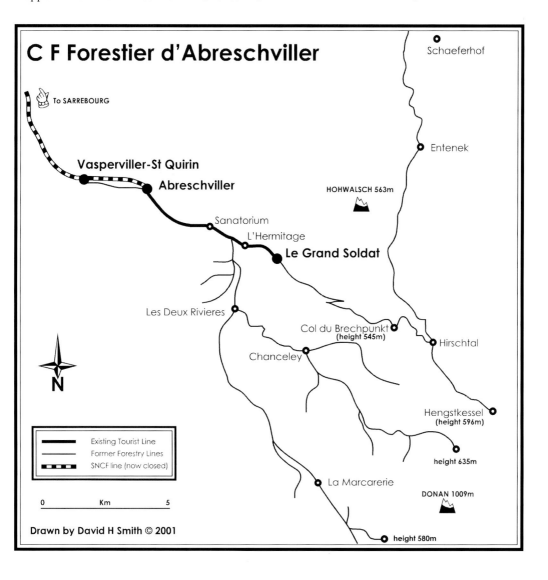

5.2.   At Grand-Soldat, the Mallet stops for water before tackling the steep climb into the forests. The current tourist line terminates a short distance beyond this point. (D.Trevor Rowe).

5.3.   During part of the journey, the Mallet was assisted by the Coferna diesel locomotive. They are seen at yet another water stop. Note the long coupling poles between the locomotives and rolling stock. These were necessary due to the length of the felled trees on the timber wagons and the excessive curvature of the line. (D.Trevor Rowe).

5.4.   Deep in the forest, a halt is made whilst discussions take place prior to the return journey. The coupling pole was made from timber. (D.Trevor Rowe).

5.5.   The track inspection vehicle based on a 1925 Renault motor vehicle is seen at Abreschviller. This interesting machine, along with a similar Hotchkiss, has been preserved by the Chemin de Fer D'Abreschviller. (D.Trevor Rowe).

top left
5.6.   Thirty five years later the Heilbronn Mallet, fresh from a major overhaul, stands outside the engine shed at Abreschviller prior to a test run on 17th July 2001. (J.F. Organ).

left
5.7.   On the same date, the Jung 0-6-0TT, acquired from Austria, prepares to haul the first train of the day to Grand-Soldat. (J.F.Organ).

lower left
5.8.   During its first "running in trip", the Mallet passes through the hamlet of Grand-Soldat. Note the hefty wooden buffer beams fitted to this interesting locomotive, which was built in 1906. (J.F. Organ).

5.9.   A few minutes later, the powerful Jung 0-6-0TT passes the same level crossing with a passenger train. This photograph makes an interesting comparison with number 5.2. (J.F. Organ).

5.10.   The two locomotives at the delightful upper terminus, a short distance beyond Grand-Soldat, on 17th July 2001. (J.F. Organ).

5.11.   *A detailed study of the Heilbronn 0-4-4-0T Mallet. Fresh from its overhaul, which included a replacement boiler, the locomotive was still in unlined primer at this time. (J.F. Organ).*

5.12.   *Two Orenstein & Koppel 0-4-0Ts and a Czechoslovakian 0-4-0T built by CKD (centre) pose at the works of Lambert Frères, Cormeilles-en-Parisis on 30th March 1961. (D.Trevor Rowe).*

5.13. O & K 0-4-0T no.3 prepares to move off the shed at Cormeilles on the same date. (D.Trevor Rowe)

5.14. The CKD 0-4-0T hauls a load of hopper wagons from the works in March 1961. Had the proposed sale not fallen through at the last moment, this locomotive would now have been hauling tourist trains between Tywyn and Nant Gwernol. (D.Trevor Rowe).

6. METRE GAUGE MISCELLANY

Following the Freycinet plan of 1880, the metre gauge network of secondary lines throughout France increased at a rapid rate. Lines of both *Intérét Général* and *Intérét Local* were constructed and opened in an attempt to provide transport needs to many hitherto isolated areas of the country. Many were independent operations, some associated with the main line companies whilst others were under the control of groups that were responsible for numerous systems. Three of the largest groups were the *Chemins de Fer Départementaux* (CFD), the *Société Général des Chemins de Fer Economiques* (SE) and *Cie Général des Vois Ferrées d'Intérêt Local* (VFIL) which controlled the majority of secondary lines between them. Whilst the CFD operated lines throughout the country, the SE and VFIL systems were mainly confined to the Northern part of France. Both the CFD and VFIL possessed extensive workshops, which in later years built numerous diesel powered locomotives and railcars.

Whilst large systems such as the CFD Réseau du Vivarais and Paris-Orléans Corrèze (POC) were typical of those in Southern France, the majority in the north were shorter lines although many were quite substantial undertakings despite their comparatively short length. One notable exception was the CF du Blanc à Argent, a 190km cross country route linking Le Blanc in Indre with Argent in Loiret. Other important lines included the CF du Cambrésis in the Nord département and the SE controlled Somme group in the département of the same name. So many were the metre gauge lines in Northern France that to describe them all in a publication of this size would be almost impossible. In addition, there were lines with similar titles, which may confuse the issue. Notable examples were the CFD Réseau de Seine-et-Marne and the SE Réseau de Seine-et-Marne whilst further south were the CFD Réseau de Saône-et-Loire and the CFIL de Saône-et-Loire. This chapter will concentrate on three notable contrasting metre gauge systems, two of which are happily still operating, plus one museum line which has preserved much equipment that would otherwise have been lost for ever.

CF du Cambrésis

Opened in 1881, this *Intérét Local* system eventually comprised of four lines which formed a cross radiating from Caudry. With a total length of 120km the four sections terminated at Cambrai, Catillon, St.Quentin and the mining town of Denain near the Belgian border. This part of the Nord Département is not exactly renowned for its scenic qualities but the CF du Cambrésis became a "mecca" for many enthusiasts prior to its closure in 1960. For almost eighty years it performed its daily duties, hauling passenger and freight trains along the four branches, connecting with the main line system at each of the terminal stations. The hub of the system at Caudry was set in a dismal industrialised area, where the headquarters of the line were established including extensive workshops and sheds.

The timetable for passenger trains was flexible to say the least. Depending upon the length of the lunch and beer stop for crew, passengers could arrive at their destination at any time to suit the operation on the day of their travel! Due to the unsavoury, or lack of, toilet facilities at stations, passengers were warned by means of enamel signs not to use the end balconies of the coaches as an alternative toilet! Freight traffic, which was the life-blood of the line, carried coal from Denain plus agricultural produce and general merchandise from the localities served by the system.

Steam reigned supreme until the end at Caudry, apart from some primitive Renault-Scémia four wheeled railcars. The latter were somewhat eclipsed by the continued use of steam traction on all but the lightest workings. The last branch to survive was the 28km route to Denain, which continued to operate both passenger and freight services until 1960. The line became a favourite destination for British enthusiasts during the final period of its operation, the surviving limb being almost a time warp unaffected by modernisation and the march of progress. The main reason for its continued existence was to convey miners to and from Denain, in addition to coal trains from the same source. Its bright green locomotives, including some of the most modern and powerful machines on the French metre gauge lines, contrasted with the drab surroundings in which they operated. Civil engineering features of the line were conspicuous by their absence, with no appreciable gradients to climb, the larger locomotives, although not overtaxed, could haul coal trains of considerable length.

The steam locomotives comprised of three basic types. The oldest were the Corpet-Louvet 0-6-0Ts supplied for the opening of the line in 1881, with further examples arriving during the following decade as the system expanded. The type of machine most associated with the Cambrésis were the Piguet 2-6-0Ts built in 1914 for the CF de la Drôme. These handsome locomotives handled freight and passenger trains, many of them mixed formations, until the end of operations in 1960. A typical combination would consist of five wooden bodied end balcony coaches marshalled behind a fourgon and two or three open goods wagons. In the time honoured fashion of mixed trains, passengers could expect many delays whilst shunting the freight stock took place en route, not to mention the aforementioned beer stops!

It has always been accepted that the last metre gauge locomotives built for use in France were the four 0-6-6-0T Mallets built by SACM in 1932 for the CFD Vivarais. However, in 1948 Corpet-Louvet built three massive 2-8-2Ts as part of an export order. Due to the cancellation of this order, these powerful locomotives were acquired by the CF du Cambrésis and used on the heavy coal trains from Denain. These handsome engines, as large as many standard gauge locomotives, must have made a wonderful sight hauling a lengthy freight train across the windswept fields of the Nord Département. Sadly an example didn't survive into preservation, even though it would have been too large and heavy to operate on many of the existing tourist lines.

Two of the Corpet-Louvet 0-6-0Ts were sold to the Waltham ironstone quarries in Leicestershire before WW 2, an unusual example of a metre gauge line in Great Britain. Named *Cambrai* and *Nantes*, the former was saved when the Waltham system closed. The preserved locomotive is in fact a combination of the best parts of the two, but carries the name *Cambrai*. During the 1960s it was displayed at Tywyn station of the Talyllyn Railway, since when it has been restored to working order and now resides at the metre gauge Irchester Railway in Northamptonshire. Sadly, this is the only surviving reminder of this typical example of a French secondary railway that served its industrial locality quietly and unobtrusively for almost eighty years.

CF du Blanc à Argent

Conceived as a standard gauge cross country strategic line as part of the Paris-Orléans empire, the intention was to link the départements of Indre, Loir et Cher and Loiret. The scheme in its original guise never progressed further than the planning stage, but the idea wasn't completely abandoned. Ultimately the PO accepted the concession to build a 190km *Intérét Général* metre gauge line to link no less than six standard gauge junctions along its route. Running from Argent in Loiret, the line ran in a south-westerly direction to Salbris, Romorantin and Gièvres which were situated in Loir et Cher and finally into Indre for the final section linking Valencay, Lucay-le-Mâle, Buzancais and Le Blanc. The system opened in 1901 with the headquarters situated conveniently in the centre of operations at Romorantin.

With such a comparatively long line, the system was divided into five sections for operating purposes. These were Argent-Salbris, Salbris-Romorantin, Romorantin-Valencay, Valencay-Buzancais and Buzancais-Le Blanc. Despite its rural location, the railway possessed some notable architectural features. Examples were the station building at Romorantin, which was built for the main line that crossed the BA at this point, and the ornate station at Valencay. The latter was completely incongruous in its surroundings, being built in the same style as the local château at the instigation and funding of the Duc de Valencay. From an engineering point of view, the line ran through pleasant but unspectacular countryside and therefore required little in the way of bridges and tunnels, whilst the steepest gradients were very modest.

In this form the line performed its unassuming but important role for the first half of the 20th Century. During WW 2 the CF du Blanc à Argent straddled between the occupied zone and the area controlled by the Vichy government. Not surprisingly, this led to the Resistance movement making use of the line for some surreptitious smuggling of arms during those dark and dangerous days. The peace of 1945 heralded a new era of line closures and cut backs, and the BA was no exception. Initially the two extreme ends of the system closed, which of course included the two towns after which the line was named. First to close was the northern link between Argent and Clémont in 1951 followed by the southern section between Le Blanc and Buzancais in 1953. There then followed a static period until 1973 when the Clémont to Salbris section succumbed to rationalisation and finally Buzancais to Lucay-le-Mâle lost its passenger service in 1980, its freight service lingering on for a few more years. The remaining 67km between Salbris and Lucay-le-Mâle continued to operate a regular passenger service connecting with the main SNCF line from Paris to Toulouse at Salbris. This section is happily still running and in recent years has been the subject of some modernisation of rolling stock. The line is now operated by Compagnie du Blanc à Argent on behalf of the SNCF.

Until the early 1950s the freight traffic, and originally passenger trains, were hauled by some modest motive power in the form of 0-6-0T and 2-4-0T locomotives built by Blanc-Misseron, Buffaud-Robatel and Batignolles. The latter were 2-4-0Ts transferred from the PO Corrèze, which was another subsidiary line of the Paris-Orléans company. The steam locomotives were notable in being fitted with large and unsightly spark arresting chimneys in deference to the woodlands and dry undergrowth alongside this rural railway. In common with its contemporary lines, railcars took over most of the passenger traffic during the 1930s. These were a fairly mixed batch although the majority were the familiar Billard and SCF-Verney units. The latter were built in 1950 and were transferred from the PO Corrèze in 1970. These five units, along with two smaller CFD cars built in 1984, are still in service and are kept in immaculate condition. Following the closure of the Réseau Breton in 1967, six De Dion Bouton type OC2 railcars were transferred to Romorantin. Numbered X201 - X206, only X202 and X205 actually entered service, the remaining four being used as a source of spare parts. X 205 remains in operation whilst X 202 has returned to Brittany for preservation.

Following the withdrawal of the steam locomotives, four CFD diesel tractors, built on the frames of redundant steam powered machines, took over the freight workings during the 1940s. These 0-6-0s proved, as on many other lines, to be very powerful and economical locomotives. Two of the BA engines, nos.11 and 12, were noted for their array of air brake cylinders on the cab roofs. Nos.13 and 14 remain at Romorantin whilst no.12 now works on the CF de Baie de la Somme.

In 2001/2, five articulated twin railcar sets are due to be delivered from CFD-Bagnères, for which a new depot and workshop has been built at Romorantin. These units of very modern appearance are intended to replace the ageing SCF-Verney railcars, which have given such sterling service for over 50 years. With investments in new rolling stock the, Blanc-Argent appears to have a secure future as a passenger carrying line. Sadly, regular freight services ceased in 1989 although the last remaining 0-6-0 Diesel locomotives have been retained for occasional work.

Although the 67km section between Salbris and Lucay-le-Mâle is the only surviving part of the original system in regular use, part of the closed section south of Lucay-le-Mâle has been taken over by a preservation group. The SABA has saved some items of redundant rolling stock, including one of the original railcars which has been restored to a high standard.

Salbris is situated approximately 50km south of Orléans on the N20 whilst Romorantin is located on the D724, 25km west of Salbris, 50km south of Orléans via the D922.

CF de la Baie de Somme

The foundations of the metre gauge Baie de Somme system, or *Réseau des Bains de Mer* as it used to be known, began in 1858 with a 4km standard gauge branch of the CF du Nord from Noyelles to St.Valery. The former is situated on the old Nord main line from Calais to Paris, a short distance to the west of Abbeville. The port of St.Valery is on the Somme estuary where the Somme Canal joins the tidal river a short distance from the quays. Its principal claim to historic fame occurred in 1066, when William of Normandy sailed from St. Valery bound for Hastings and a confrontation with King Harold.

Although the standard gauge branch achieved its aim of connecting the port to the main line system, following *Le Plan Freycinet* of 1880 it was thought desirable to extend the line on both sides of the Somme estuary. A continuation of the standard gauge was considered too expensive but a metre gauge line was a far more viable proposition. Consequently the SE obtained a 99 year concession in 1884 to construct and operate an *Intérét Local* line to connect the coastal resorts of Le Crotoy and Cayeux with Noyelles. However, the Noyelles to St.Valery section retained its *Intérét Général* status, with separate tickets being issued for that part of the route. Ultimately, this relatively short line became part of the much larger SE Réseau de la Somme incorporating ten lines throughout the département with a total distance of 329km.

The 6km line along the northern side of the estuary to Le Crotoy began operations on 1st July 1887. Initially the route ran parallel to the standard gauge branch from Noyelles before diverting to the right and following a rural course alongside fields a short distance inland from the sand banks of the Somme estuary. After a succession of level crossings over minor roads and farm tracks, the terminus on the outskirts of Le Crotoy embraced a two storey station building and engine shed, so typical of the structures at similar locations throughout France.

On 6th September 1887 the 19km line from Noyelles to Cayeux was opened. Cayeux is situated on the Channel coast south of the Somme estuary. For the first 4km to St.Valery Canal, the metre gauge track was interlaced with the standard gauge, a situation that has survived to the present day. Unlike the normal arrangement with a third rail inserted between the standard gauge rails, the dual gauge on the Somme utilised four rails with the metre gauge tracks wholly within the standard gauge rails. This section was originally carried across the head of the bay on a long wooden viaduct. This was replaced in 1911 by a solid embankment, which ultimately contributed to the silting up of the estuary. From St.Valery Canal the metre gauge track crossed the canal lock over a swing bridge before arriving at the new station of St.Valery Ville near the quayside. Here a short spur ran off to the right, terminating on the quays near the town centre. The line to Cayeux swung off to the left before ascending a steep climb to the plateau south of St.Valery. The principal intermediate station was at Lancheres where a sugar refinery was situated. This had its own internal system with two locomotives, which occasionally travelled to Noyelles with loaded trains of beet.

In addition to its role as a resort, Cayeux was noted for its high quality flint pebbles, which were used extensively in the production of concrete by the construction industry. This provided continual traffic throughout the year, unlike the largely seasonal passenger traffic. The layout at Cayeux was similar to that at Le Crotoy apart from extra sidings, necessary for handling the heavy stone traffic.

Following the opening of the metre gauge line to St.Valery, the CF du Nord ceased to operate passenger trains and locomotives on their standard gauge branch. Henceforth, standard gauge goods wagons were hauled by metre gauge locomotives, a practice which continued until 1973. The original station at St.Valery Canal was relegated to a halt, being replaced by a larger two storey station building on the quayside named St.Valery Ville. During both world wars, the line was in the forefront of battle being of strategic importance to the Allies during the first conflict, whilst the occupying forces made good use of it during WW2 to transport materials for the construction of block-houses which formed part of the "Atlantic Wall".

During the days of peace, the *Réseau des Bains de Mer* (the Sea Bathers Railway) operated consistently heavy passenger trains, particularly during the summer, along with a substantial freight traffic. The latter was mainly flint pebbles from Cayeux and sugar beet from Lancheres, together with items of agricultural and general merchandise. In addition to the two coastal routes, a third line from Noyelles climbed alongside the main line to the north of the station before crossing the latter at a higher level. This line, which closed for passengers in 1951, ran inland to Forest l'Abbaye where it connected with another metre gauge line that ran from Abbeville to Dompierre-sur-Authie.

In 1961, the SE became part of the *Compagnie Général de Chemins de Fer et des Transport Automobile* (CFTA), the new organisation inheriting the operation of the Somme system. With an interest in both rail and road transport, the CFTA soon began to investigate economical cut backs and rationalisation. Consequently the traffic steadily declined during the 1960s until the Le Crotoy line closed on 31st December 1969. The Cayeux line survived slightly longer, the last trains running until 31st December 1972. However, a preservation society had already been formed and trains had once again been running to Le Crotoy prior to the closure of the Cayeux line.

Locomotives and rolling stock

During the early years of the CF de la Baie de Somme, a number of SACM 0-6-2T locomotives drawn from the SE stock were used on the line. During the late 1940s these were largely replaced by a fleet of 2-6-0Ts, built in Belgium in 1921 by Haine-St.Pierre. Locomotives of both types were freely exchanged with other lines in the SE empire, the branch to Forest l'Abbaye providing a metre gauge connection with other lines in the Somme area. During the 1940s, a small number of diverse locomotives were transferred from other SE operated lines, principally the Réseau Centre.

In order to haul standard gauge wagons, some of the Somme locomotives were equipped with twin buffers in addition to the usual metre gauge central buffer.

Railcars made an appearance on passenger trains during 1935 with the introduction of some De Dion Bouton type NJ four wheeled cars and a type NR bogie unit. In 1955 three VFIL machines, built in 1936 for the Flandres network, were added to the stock. From the same source, these were joined by two 1951 built VFIL diesel locomotives in 1957. Rather than fitting these with twin buffers, for hauling standard gauge rolling stock, a metre gauge wagon fitted with a combination of twin and single buffers and couplings was employed between the diesel locomotives and standard gauge stock.

Passenger rolling stock comprised 19 wooden bodied end balcony coaches built by Manage in Belgium. In addition were three baggage wagons (fourgons) and large stock of open and covered freight vehicles. In 1958 the freight stock totalled 310 items including 61closed, 78 open and 171 skip wagons. As late as 1971, one of De Dion Bouton type OC1 railcars, formerly employed in Brittany, was transferred to the Somme, which has remained on the line.

The Preservation Era

As recorded above, a scheme to save the Le Crotoy branch was instigated shortly after that line closed in 1969. The decision to form the *Association du Chemin de Fer de la Baie de Somme* (CFBS) was made in November of that year, whilst its constitution officially began in March 1970. With assistance from FACS, an industrial 0-4-0T built by Corpet-Louvet in 1925 was acquired to operate the initial trains, the former stock of Somme steam locomotives having already been withdrawn. Following the usual never ending discussions with the relevant authorities, services finally began on 4th July 1971. Two more Corpet-Louvet 0-4-0Ts arrived from the same source during that year, one of which was used for spare parts. Meanwhile the association had inherited the rolling stock that remained on the line following the CFTAs closure, plus the two VFIL diesel locomotives and surviving railcars. The Corpet-Louvet industrial locomotives are very low in relation to the carriages and have gained the affectionate name of *les Teckels* (the Dachshunds). This height difference is most notable when travelling on the end balcony of the leading coach of a train hauled by one of these small machines. From that vantage point, one can enjoy a clear view of the road ahead, looking over the cab and boiler fittings of the locomotive. The drawback to this interesting spectacle is that the exhaust from the chimney is inconveniently at eye level!

With the closure of the Cayeux line in December 1972, ambitious plans were announced to extend operations to cover the entire surviving system. Additional locomotives arrived including a 1904 Pinguely 0-6-0T from CF du Morbihan, a unique 1909 Buffaud & Robatel 0-6-2T from the SE Seine and Marne line, a 1906 Corpet-Louvet 2-6-0T from Ainse and a 1920 built Haine-St.Pierre 2-6-0T from the VFIL, similar to the final steam locomotives employed on the Somme system. More recent acquisitions have included a 2-6-0T built by Cail in 1889 for use on the Panama Canal railway. Having spent many years in various museums in the USA, this interesting locomotive arrived back on its native soil in 1994. Additions to the diesel stock have included a CFD 0-6-0 from the CF du Blanc à Argent and a powerful Naval built machine from Spain.

Additional passenger stock acquired from Switzerland arrived during the 1970s to relieve the ailing original stock which was in dire need of overhaul. These have been joined in later years by other items of rolling stock, mainly from Switzerland, although some items of French origin such as the Réseau Breton have also been acquired.

Despite this ongoing activity, there was dissent below the surface. Whilst the CFBS were operating trains to Le Crotoy and St.Valery, the line from St.Valery to Cayeux was taken over by a splinter group in 1975 who wished to operate the railway on a more commercial basis. This short lived venture floundered after less than two years and the diesel operated service on the Cayeux line ceased to run after 1977, when the entire system reverted to CFBS control.

Since those early problems, the CF de la Baie de Somme has gone from strength to strength and is now one of the principal tourist railways of France. With a progressive track renewal programme completed and passenger numbers in excess of 80,000 per year, it is a professionally run operation despite its heavy reliance on volunteer labour. Unlike many French tourist lines, a daily service is operated throughout the Summer period supported by a weekend and limited daily service during Spring and Autumn. Steam is used on the Le Crotoy and St.Valery services whilst the less intensive Cayeux service relies mainly on diesel haulage. On special occasions, such as gala events, steam haulage is used on the entire system.

One of the highlights of the operation is the twice daily parallel departure from Noyelles. The trains for Le Crotoy and St.Valery leave the main line station simultaneously, running alongside each other until the two tracks diverge towards their respective destinations. In fact, to describe this as a parallel departure is not quite correct. The Le Crotoy train leaves a few seconds before, being overtaken by the St.Valery train where the division of the tracks is reached, accompanied by the usual French passion of much whistling from the locomotives and cheerful banter from the passengers!

The majority of journeys along the line begin from the principal station at St.Valery, even though Noyelles is located at the hub of the system. Although St.Valery Ville station is located alongside the junction of the Cayeux line, the spur to the quayside is the normal point of departure. From this delightful position, the line runs alongside the road and river before swinging around a long curve to cross the canal by the aforementioned swing bridge, which is also used by road traffic. Shortly after crossing the bridge, the extensive workshops and locomotive depot at St.Valery Canal are passed. Since the CFBS assumed control, these have been enlarged with capacity for complete restoration and rebuilding of locomotives and rolling stock. The remainder of the journey to Noyelles is mainly on the embankment constructed across the head of the estuary, until the Le Crotoy line appears from the north and runs alongside the mixed gauge track for the final part of the journey into Noyelles. The layout at Noyelles comprises two platforms and a number of sidings of both metre and standard gauges situated alongside the main line station.

From Noyelles one can travel alongside the northern side of the estuary to Le Crotoy or retrace the route to St.Valery and thence to Cayeux. The Cayeux line begins with a fairly steep incline, which has been known to tax some of the less powerful steam locomotives. Following the summit of the climb, the line runs across the wide expanse of plateau leading towards the coast. A number of level crossings are passed and the remains of the sugar refinery at Lancheres which is now an agricultural depot. The station at Cayeux is located near the centre of this popular resort, which incorporates a beach known as Brighton Plage.

Situated on the English Channel Coast approximately mid way between Calais and Dieppe, the CF de la Baie de Somme is the most easily accessible of the surviving French narrow gauge lines for visitors from Great Britain. It is also possible to travel there by rail. Although the "old" main line from Calais to Paris has been relegated to secondary status since the opening of the Channel Tunnel and the new TGV line, a reasonable service still operates to Noyelles, which is served by local trains between Calais and Amiens.

A visit is highly recommended to this fascinating line, which provides a lasting reminder of a typical example of the numerous rural metre gauge railways that were once so common throughout France. St.Valery and Noyelles are both situated on the D940 coast road between Le Tréport and Le Touquet.

Musée des Transports de la Vallée du Sausseron

One of the many smaller metre gauge lines operated by the SE ran from Valmondois to Marines, about 35km north of Paris. Running along the delightful valley of the River Oise and its tributary the Sausseron, the 15km line existed quietly between 1891 and 1949, acting as a feeder to other railways in the area controlled by the SE. These included the standard gauge branches from Magny-en-Vexin to Chars and Chars to Marines, all of which had closed by the early 1950s.

In 1976 a museum devoted to the narrow gauge railways of the area was established at the old abandoned depot at Valmondois. Adopting the name of *Musée de Transports de la Vallée du Sausseron* (MTVS), the initial locomotives and rolling stock comprised of items from both 60cm and metre gauge systems. Ultimately the 60cm equipment was to form the nucleus of the Chanteraines collection, being transferred to the CFC by 1991. Meanwhile the metre gauge collection at Valmondois continued to expand whilst a 1km demonstration line was constructed along the track bed of the old line to Marines. In 1998 the organisation changed its name, whilst retaining its initials MTVS. It is now known as *Le Musée des Tramways a Vapeur et des Chemins de Fer Secondaires Francais* (The French Local Trains and Steam Tramways Museum) which is regarded as a more accurate description of its activities.

Since its inception, the MTVS collection has continued to increase and currently totals nine steam locomotives, five diesel units and about twenty items of rolling stock. Acquired from various sources throughout France, and in one case Portugal, many of the exhibits arrived in a very poor condition and have been painstakingly restored in the fully equipped workshops that have been developed at the depot.

It had always been the intention of the museum to extend the running line along the former track bed towards Marines. However, residential developments in the area have prevented any extension of the current demonstration line. In order to overcome this, a dramatic solution has been decided upon in which the whole operation will move to a new site at Chars. The new location will provide far more scope for expansion with part of the old standard gauge route between Chars and Magny-en-Vexin being available for an extended operating line. Negotiations with the relevant authorities are taking place at the time of writing (2001) and it is hoped that the MTVS will be transferred to the new location during 2003.

Locomotives and Rolling Stock

The first steam locomotive to arrive in 1976 was a 0-6-0TR Twin Cab tramway locomotive from the Tramways de la Sarthe, a product of Blanc-Misseron in 1898. This delightful machine was reunited with a similar locomotive, also from the Sarthe Tramway, in 1987. During the 1980s a number of larger locomotives were added to the collection. In 1981 a powerful 2-6-0T built by Orenstein & Koppel in 1913 (as part of a sub-contract order from Decauville) arrived from the Val de Vouga line in Portugal. This large machine,

which is currently on static display in the museum, was subsequently joined in 1984 and 1988 by a pair of Corpet-Louvet 0-6-0Ts from the CF Côtes-du-Nord (1925) and Tramways d'Ille et Vilaine (1909) respectively. 1990 saw the arrival of a Pinguely 0-6-0T built in 1897 for the CF de la Drôme and a SACM 2-6-0T dating from 1924 which spent its working life on the CGL Pas de Calais line. Two interesting smaller exhibits include a diminutive industrial 0-4-0T built by Corpet-Louvet and a vertical boiler 0-4-0T built by Cockerill in 1908.

The diesel powered stock includes two of the well known CFD 0-6-0 loco-tractors built in 1948 as rebuilds of retired steam locomotives. These both began life as Corpet-Louvet products, originally built for the CF du Doubs, as 2-6-0T and 0-6-0T locomotives. The former subsequently saw service on the CFD du Tarn whilst the other unit worked on the Voies Ferrées du Dauphiné. These powerful locomotives have been joined by two smaller industrial loco-tractors, and a diesel-electric machine built by Brissoneau and Lotz in 1937.

The rolling stock includes examples of both

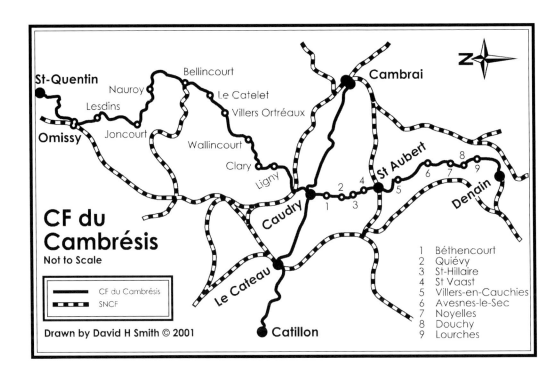

CF du Cambrésis

Not to Scale

| | CF du Cambrésis |
| | SNCF |

Drawn by David H Smith © 2001

1 Béthencourt
2 Quiévy
3 St-Hillaire
4 St Vaast
5 Villers-en-Cauchies
6 Avesnes-le-Sec
7 Noyelles
8 Douchy
9 Lourches

four wheeled and bogie coaches from a large variety of former railways throughout France. The majority of these date from the 19th century, the youngest example being built in 1913. In addition three of the ubiquitous fourgons (luggage vans), that were such a familiar feature of the French railways, have joined the collection along with a representative collection of freight stock.

Much of the collection is classed as *Monument Historique,* which allows financial aid from the State to be obtained for their restoration and continued maintenance. The immaculate presentation of the stock, and the continued restoration to an equally high standard, reflects this invaluable contribution. The MTVS, which is currently situated at Valmondais (near Butry sur Oise) contains one of the finest representative collections of metre gauge locomotives and rolling stock in France. Its close proximity to Paris is of great advantage for potential visitors, although it is only open at weekends and bank holidays.

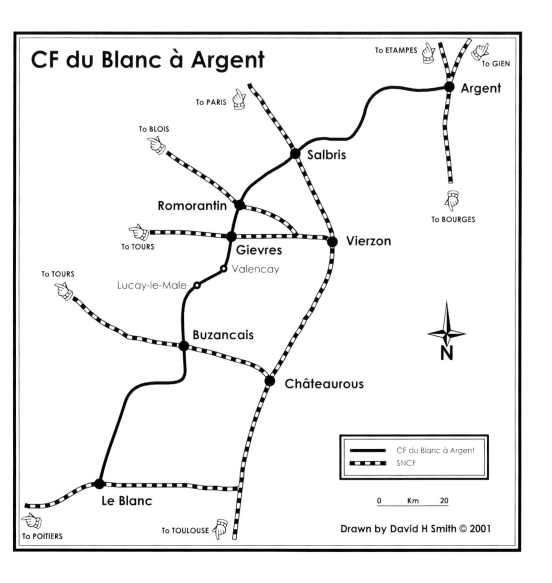

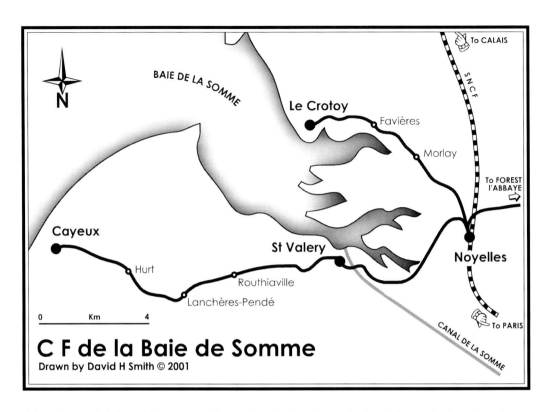

6.1.   Piguet 2-6-0T no.30 prepares to depart from Caudry with a mixed train bound for Denain on the CF du Cambrésis in 1956. (B. Rozé / BVA).

6.2.   The same locomotive leaves Denain with the 14.25 to Caudry on 4th September 1957.
(B. Rozé / BVA).

6.3.   This is one of the Piguet 2-6-0Ts, that were associated with the Cambrésis for many years. No.35 is
seen at Caudry depot in 1955.   *(M.Rifault. Coll.- J.L.Rochaix / BVA).*

6.4. The three Corpet-Louvet 2-8-2Ts, constructed in 1948, were the largest locomotives used on the CFC. One of these handsome machines, no.40, was photographed at Caudry in 1955. (M.Rifault. Coll. J.L.Rochaix / BVA).

6.5. Although steam remained in daily use until the end, some 4 wheeled Renault-Scémia railcars were used on lighter duties. No.13 is seen at Caudry on 4th September 1957. (B. Rozé / BVA).

6.6.   The Blanc-Argent steam locomotives were noted for their large and unsightly spark arresting chimneys. Buffaud-Robatel 0-6-0T no.29 was viewed at Romorantin depot in 1951. (M.Rifault.   Coll.- J.L.Rochaix / BVA).

6.7.   This former POC Batignolles 2-4-0T didn't escape the same treatment after it was transferred from Tulle to Romorantin, where it was noted in 1953. (M.Rifault.   Coll.- J.L.Rochaix / BVA).

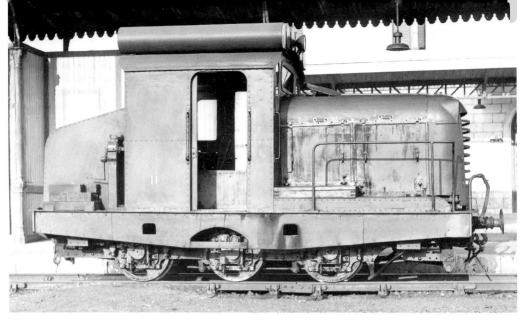

top left
6.8.   CFD 0-6-0 Loco-Tractor no. BA 11 was at Romorantin in 1954. Note the array of air brake cylinders on the cab roof. (M. Rifault.   Coll.- J.L.Rochaix / BVA).

left
6.9.   SCF-Verney railcar no.221 arrives at Salbris on 28th July 1962. (D.Trevor Rowe).

lower left
6.10.   Former Réseau Breton De Dion Bouton type OC2 railcar X205 and former POC SCF-Verney railcar 212 wait at Salbris on 2nd May 1999. The former vehicle is retained for enthusiasts specials. (D.Trevor Rowe).

6.11.   The De Dion railcar awaits its next duty at Romorantin on 20th July 2001. The large station building originally served both the metre gauge Blanc-Argent and the now closed SNCF standard gauge line.   (J.F. Organ).

6.12.   SCF-Verney railcars 224 and 212 are seen at Romorantin on 20th July 2001. 212 was extensively refurbished in 1984, hence the modified appearance. (J.F. Organ).

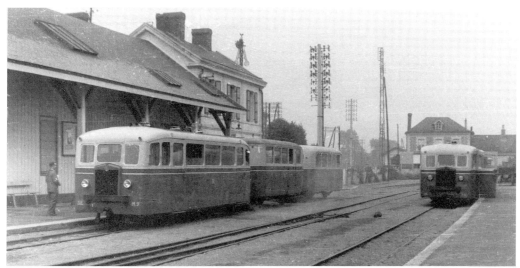

top left
6.13. CFD diesel loco-tractors BA 13 and BA 14 rest at Romorantin in July 2001. Although regular freight traffic ceased in 1989, these machines are retained for occasional use. (J.F. Organ).

left
6.14. Railcar no.212 arrives at Valencay on 21st July 2001 with a Saturday morning "shoppers train" from Salbris. (J.F. Organ).

lower left
6.15. The ornate station at Valencay has CFD railcar no.241 in attendance, on 20th July 2001. The station is built in the same style as the nearby château. (J.F. Organ).

6.16. De Dion Bouton type NR railcars are at Noyelles on the CF de la Baie de Somme on 28th August 1955. Behind the station building is the "old" Nord main line between Paris and Calais. (D. Trevor Rowe).

6.17. Haine-St.Pierre 2-6-0T no.3853 replenishes its water tanks at Noyelles in 1951. This was the hub of the system and was a very busy station in the heyday of the line.
(M.Rifault. Coll.- J.L.Rochaix / BVA).

top left
6.18.   *VFIL diesel locomotive no.351 shunts wagons at St.Valery Canal on 9th November 1963. Note the overgrown state of the permanent way at that period. (D.Trevor Rowe).*

left
6.19.   *The sugar refinery at Lancheres had its own internal system. Its two locomotives, a Corpet-Louvet 0-6-0T and an O & K 0-6-0T were photographed on 9th November 1963. (D.Trevor Rowe).*

lower left
6.20.   *Former CF du Morbihan Pinguely 0-6-0T no.101 arrives at Noyelles on 4th June 1978. By this time, the rejuvenated railway had become well established as a tourist line. (D.Trevor Rowe).*

6.21.   *Buffaud & Robatel 0-6-2T no.3714 draws into St.Valery Quay with a train from Noyelles on 14th April 2000. This must rank as one of the most delightfully situated stations in France. (J.F. Organ).*

6.22.   *Haine St.Pierre 2-6-0T no.15 drifts across the swing bridge at St.Valery prior to its days duties on 15th April 2000. (J.F. Organ).*

6.23.   Corpet-Louvet 2-6-0T no.1 storms up the incline out of St.Valery with a train bound for Cayeux on 15th April 2000.   Steam haulage is normally only used on the Cayeux line on special occasions.
(J.F. Organ).

6.24.   No.15 crosses an ungated level crossing, heading a train for Cayeux on 14th April 2000. Compared to the surroundings of the Somme Estuary, the landscape on the plateau is very bleak and windswept.
(J.F. Organ).

6.25.   *Blanc-Misseron 0-6-0TR from the Tramways de la Sarthe, with a coach from the same source, is at the MTVS depot at Valmondois on 28ᵗʰ May 1994.   (D.Trevor Rowe).*

6.26.   *A Decauville 2-6-0T, built by O &K in 1913 and repatriated from Portugal, is seen in the museum at Valmondois in 1994. This metre gauge locomotive has all the hallmarks of the smaller Decauville products. (D.Trevor Rowe).*

6.27.   In the museum on 15th July 2001 was Pinguely 0-6-0T no.16, with the Brissoneau and Lotz diesel-electric locomotive behind. (J.F. Organ).

6.28.   Former CdN Corpet-Louvet 0-6-0T no.36 prepares to collect the passenger stock prior to the first train of the day on 15th July 2001. (J.F. Organ).

7.   METRE GAUGE IN BRITTANY

The Breton Peninsular used to boast the highest concentration of metre gauge railways in France. Among the five systems that at one time traversed the three départements of Finistère, Côtes du Nord and Morbihan were two of the largest narrow gauge networks, the Réseau Breton (RB) and CF des Côtes-du-Nord (CdN). These have both tended to overshadow the three less known systems, the CFD du Finistère (CFDF), CF Armoricains (CFA) and CF du Morbihan (CM).

The CFDF was an *Intérét Local* system in the north-west of Brittany which was opened in stages between 1893 and 1907. Its main route ran from Brest to St Pol de Léon (near Roscoff) with branches to the coastal towns of Porspoder, L'Aberwrach and Brignogan. There was also a short isolated branch in the south-west running from Concarneau to Quimperle. Although scheduled for closure during the late 1930s, following the nationalisation of the French railways, most of the system was reprieved during WW 2 under the control of the state owned Réseau Breton. With the onset of peace, the CFDF passed into history in 1946.

The CFA was another *Intérét Local* line that ran from Plouescat on the north coast to Rosporden, which was the southern terminus of the Réseau Breton. Another shorter section ran from Morlaix to Plestin Les Greves, where it connected with the CdN, with a branch to Primel Tregastel. Opened in 1912, the CFA was absorbed into the CFDF in 1921, the two systems thereafter being operated as one. The Rosporden line closed in 1934 as a result of competition from the RB and road transport.

The remainder was closed in 1946 along with the surviving CFDF lines.

The CM was a sprawling *Intérét Local* system in the département of Morbihan. Opened in stages between 1902 and 1921, it comprised of a total route mileage of 433km in its final form. The main route ran from Gourin to La Roche Bernard via Meslan, Lochmine and Vannes. A northern route left the main route at Meslan running to Pontivy and Ploermel whilst further branches reached Port Louis and Port Navalo on the south coast of Brittany. Although railcars were introduced in 1931, the majority of passenger services were replaced by buses the following year, with much of the system closing by 1939. The war saved the principal routes from immediate closure although this was quickly implemented afterwards, the remaining lines being closed in 1947. However two of the line's Pinguely 0-6-0Ts have survived as a reminder of the CM. No. 101 now works on the CF de la Baie de Somme whilst 103 stands on a plinth near the river at Tournon where it serves as a "three dimensional" advertisement for the nearby CF du Vivarais.

CF des Côtes-du-Nord

The concession to construct this *Intérét Local* system was awarded to the *Compagnie Côtes-du-Nord* in 1900. With its headquarters at St.Brieuc, the initial lines were opened in 1905 to connect the latter town with Rostrenen to the south-west, Paimpol and Lannion on the north coast plus an isolated branch from Plancoet to Lancieux in the east of the département. Due to the rugged nature of the north coast of Brittany, many substantial civil engineering structures were required to traverse the numerous estuaries and inlets between Paimpol and Lannion. These included two suspension bridges and many viaducts, which saw an early use of reinforced concrete. This coastal section was one of the most scenic railway routes in Northern France. The majority of station buildings were fairly modest affairs with the notable exception of the monumental station, with its ornate overall curved roof, at St.Brieuc Centrale. Other notable civil engineering features were constructed at St.Brieuc. Upon leaving the Gare de Centrale, the line was carried along the hillside on a series of reinforced concrete buttressed viaducts. There then followed the huge "double decked" *Viaduc du Souzin,* on the Paimpol line, which included a junction at its northern end where a short branch to La Phare diverged to the east. When the system was extended another large viaduct, the *Viaduc du Toupin,* was constructed near St.Brieuc immediately after the line towards St Cast deviated from the above mentioned buttressed structures.

In 1909 a concession was granted for the CdN to construct additional lines to the system. These included a line running south from St.Brieuc to Loudeac, with a branch leaving that line at Plemy running east to Dinan. The isolated branch to Plancoet was connected to the remainder of the system via a line around the north-east coast whilst short branches were built to Plestin Les Greves (where it connected with the CFA line from Morlaix), Perros Guirrec, Pleubian, St Cast and

Quintin. Although construction began in earnest, most of the projects were delayed by WW 1 with the result that the CdN in its final form wasn't completed until 1926. By this time the original company had found itself in financial difficulties resulting in a joint administration with the département being formed in 1922. With a total length of 457km running through many small communities and few large centres, this was obviously not an economical operation.

Despite the early introduction of railcars during the late 1920s, it was still proving difficult to run a profitable service. The first closures took place in 1937 and by 1939 only the original line from St.Brieuc to Lannion plus two branches to Pleubian and Perros Guirrec was left, a distance of about 100km. WW 2 saw the reopening of some of the lines to the north-east of St.Brieuc but following the Allied invasions in 1944 much of the system suffered much irreparable damage and was closed permanently. By 1950 only the most successful route, the 43km from St.Brieuc to Paimpol, survived. This coastal route became a magnet for British enthusiasts during early 1950s until it too was closed on December 31st 1956. The final humiliation was the conversion of the impressive station at St.Brieuc Centrale into a bus terminus!

Locomotives and Rolling Stock.

The first locomotives to be supplied to the CdN in 1905 were seventeen 0-6-0Ts built by Blanc-Misseron. These were fitted with deep buffer beams and full side skirting enclosing the wheels and motion in view of the roadside nature of much of the early route. However the locomotives most associated with the CdN were the Corpet-Louvet 0-6-0Ts built at various times between 1908 and 1925. During that period a total of sixteen of these handsome locomotives were supplied and the maroon livery suited their attractive appearance. Unlike the earlier machines, these were of conventional design with exposed wheels and motion. Obviously the fear of causing injury and damage to road users had proved to be unfounded.

One of the later members of the class, no.36, was displayed on a plinth at St.Brieuc during the years following closure of the CdN. Having suffered from exposure to the elements and vandalism, the Corpet-Louvet was removed in 1971. Initially it was intended for use on an abortive tourist line at the CFD Lozère. The failure of that scheme saw no.36 stored in the locomotive

depot at Longueville. In 1984 it was transferred to the MTVS at Valmondois where it has been beautifully restored to its former glory and returned to working order.

As mentioned above, the CdN was an early user of railcars for many of its passenger services. In 1923 no fewer than eleven primitive De Dion Bouton JM series four-wheeled cars were supplied. These were basically single deck buses converted for rail use. Their success resulted in three of the superior KG models joining the fleet in 1927. These six-wheeled vehicles were often to be seen towing a two-wheeled trailer car. However in 1937 these early examples were joined by two De Dion type OC1 double-ended bogie railcars of much more modern design. They were supplemented by a large Renault bogie railcar, which gained the "nickname" of *Mamm-Goz* (Grandma) by the operating staff. Renault also supplied the last railcars for the CdN in the immediate post war years with three of the impressive ABH6 vehicles, similar to those delivered to Provence. To replace the earlier De Dions, six Brissoneau-et-Lotz diesel-electric cars were also acquired second hand during the late 1940s.

Both of the De Dion OC1 machines have survived. After closure of the CdN they were transferred to the Réseau Breton. Following the closure of the RB, X157 was transferred to the Baie de Somme where it still resides whilst X158 went to Corsica. Subsequently this railcar returned home and is now preserved by the Association des Chemins de Fer des Côtes-du-Nord at Langueux, near St.Brieuc.

The rolling stock consisted of bogie coaches with end balconies, similar to the vehicles used on many other contemporary lines throughout France. The freight stock comprised the usual mixture of open and closed wagons, with examples of four wheeled and bogie vehicles. The freight traffic was largely agricultural produce plus general merchandise and fuel. With the early introduction of railcars, many of the passenger coaches passed to other railways. The remaining vehicles were retained for mixed trains and, in the latter years of the CdN, the numerous steam hauled special trains that operated between St.Brieuc and Paimpol.

Réseau Breton

Following *Le Plan Freycinet* in 1880, the concession to build an *Intérét Général* system to serve central Brittany was offered to the *Compagnie des Chemins de Fer de l'Quest.* In view of the terrain and projected traffic potential, it was agreed to construct the system to metre gauge although provision was made for an easy conversion to standard gauge should the need arise. Therefore the maximum gradients were 1 in 50 and the tight curves normally associated with narrow gauge lines were eliminated. Although the administrative headquarters of the RB was based at Morlaix, the hub of the system was the market town of Carhaix. Here were established the large workshops and principal locomotive and rolling stock depot for this extensive railway.

Built in stages, the system comprised five lines radiating from Carhaix. In 1891 the first section from Carhaix to Morlaix was opened, a distance of 49km. At the northern terminus, the metre gauge joined the standard gauge CF l'Quest line, the dual gauge track running over the lofty viaduct that spanned the fishing port of Morlaix. 1893 saw the 53km line from Carhaix to Guingamp open whilst the following year this was extended a further 37km to Paimpol. With the northern branches in operation, the 50km line south to Rosporden began operations in 1896, with a connection to the Paris Orléans line at the southern terminus. Between 1898 and 1902 the 72km line eastwards from Carhaix to Loudéac was built in stages, with a further 58km extension to La Brohinière completed in 1904. Meanwhile a western extension from Carhaix to Châteaulin, a distance of 57km was constructed between 1893 and 1904. Ultimately this line was extended a further 52km during 1923 and 1925 when the final link between Châteaulin and Camaret, plus a short branch to Le Fret was added, its construction having been delayed by WW 1. This resulted in a complete route distance of 428km.

The infrastructure of the system was fairly modest, mainly as a result of it being built to standard gauge dimensions. The largest structure was the high "double decked" viaduct at Morlaix. However this wasn't strictly part of the RB, having been built by the CF l'Quest as part of their Paris to Brest line. On the RB proper, the 11 arch curved viaduct at Châteaulin was the largest structure. Another similar viaduct crossed the River Trieux at Pontrieux on the Paimpol line, whilst a number of lattice girder bridges were used elsewhere. The stations were modest buildings, similar to those elsewhere in France, although many were built in traditional Breton architectural style. The notable exception was the large station at Carhaix, which incorporated a hotel. Also at Carhaix were the extensive workshops and locomotive depot, all contained in one large building. These were served

by nine tracks, plus a traverser providing access to the carriage repair shops. Across the tracks from the station was a large goods shed whilst sidings sprouted throughout the entire complex.

Although the concession for the RB had been granted to the CF l'Quest, the operation was handed over to the SE. This meant that the CF l'Quest owned the infrastructure, whilst the locomotives, rolling stock and buildings were leased to the SE. Part of the reason for this arrangement was the precarious financial position of the CF l'Quest. In 1909 the situation had become critical and the company was taken over by the state, thus becoming the CF de l'ETAT (State Railway), the first railway in France to be nationalised. Despite this change of ownership, the SE continued to operate the Réseau Breton with the aid of state subsidies. In 1963 the SE was absorbed into the CFTA, which has continued to operate the remaining limb of the system on behalf of the SNCF to the present day.

The various routes of the RB were through rural areas with differing scenic attributes. The Morlaix line ran a mainly twisting course through woodland whilst the Rosporden route ran over open countryside. The Guingamp line was constructed through fertile agricultural land whilst the extension to Paimpol was one of the most scenic sections, running high on a ledge above the River Trieux. Eastwards to Loudéac and La Brohinière was again mainly through an agricultural landscape whilst the line west to the coast at Camaret was probably the most interesting section. Initially it ran parallel to the Rosporden line, following the Nantes-Brest canal as far as Port de Carhaix, where the two lines diverged. At Châteaulin the line descended towards the River Aulne which was crossed by a curved 11 arch viaduct immediately after leaving Châteaulin Ville station. There then followed a steep climb to the PO station at Châteaulin Embranchement. Having crossed the PO standard gauge track on the level, the route continued across open countryside until the busy fishing port of Camaret was reached.

In 1924 the section between Guingamp and Paimpol was converted to dual gauge in order that standard gauge stock could be transported directly to the busy port of Paimpol from the ETAT Paris to Brest line at Guingamp. The metre gauge was left in place so that through working from the remainder of the RB could continue, whilst Paimpol was also served by the CdN. With a decrease in traffic following WW 2, the inner third rail was lifted in 1953 leaving the section as a purely standard gauge line which is still in use today. During its dual gauge period, this section of the RB included a peculiar "kink" in the metre gauge track. As a result of the gangers working simultaneously from each end, and the platform positions at their starting points, the two teams had laid the third rail on their respective left-hand sides, consequently resulting in a strange track layout where they met!

Other economics implemented by the SE saw the usual introduction of railcars for the majority of passenger services during the 1930s, although this wasn't fully realised until after WW 2. The post war years saw the Loudéac to La Brohinière line being reduced to a freight only service, whilst the Morlaix line saw a reduction in its service with much of its traffic being sent by road.

During the 1960s, the continued operation of the Réseau Breton was being questioned as a viable proposition. In addition to its mainly metre gauge track, and consequent transhipment of stock, the locomotives and rolling stock were rapidly becoming life expired. With the system now under the control of the CFTA, which also had interests in road transport, it was not surprising that some form of co-ordination would follow. Proposals were made to convert much of the system to standard gauge, having originally been built with this possibility in mind. However the end result was that only the Carhaix to Guingamp line, which carried the heaviest traffic, was converted to standard gauge in 1967 and along with the Paimpol line became the sole surviving section of the RB. The remainder of the system closed between April and October 1967, with CFTA buses replacing the passenger services. This 90km route from Carhaix to Paimpol is still in operation under the control of the CFTA. The workshop and depot buildings at Carhaix remain in use as a combined CFTA railcar and bus depot.

Locomotives and Rolling Stock

As one of the largest narrow gauge systems in France, it was appropriate that the Réseau Breton should operate some of the largest locomotives. However the first machines supplied in 1892 were quite modest affairs. Nine 2-4-0Ts built by SACM at Belfort (nos. E201-E 209) arrived in time for the opening of the line. These were joined in 1897 by seven similar locomotives (nos. E210-E216) built by Franco-Belge at Raismes. These small locomotives were endowed with excellent acceleration and could haul the lightweight trains prevalent at the time of their introduction. However they were not entirely suitable for freight trains, so much so that three SACM 0-6-2Ts (nos. E301-E303) were also supplied in 1892. These three locomotives soon proved incapable of handling the increasing freight traffic with the result that more powerful machines were acquired during 1895/6. These took the form of seven 0-4-4-0T Mallets built by SACM (nos. E401-E407), a larger version of the first Mallets supplied to the Réseau du Vivarais in 1890. The Mallets proved to be highly successful and continued to be used on freight trains for many years. All of the 2-4-0T, 0-6-2T and 0-4-4-0T classes were withdrawn between 1942 and 1956, by which time railcars had replaced steam haulage on the majority of passenger trains.

The second generation of RB locomotive power arrived in 1904 with five handsome 4-6-0Ts built by Franco-Belge (nos. E321-E325). In 1909 a further seven locomotives to the same design (E326-E332) were supplied by Fives-Lille. These superb machines were specifically intended for passenger trains, for which they were ideally suited. In later years they proved equally at home hauling some of the lighter freight trains and the entire class survived until closure in 1967. Two of the later batch survived into preservation. E327 now works on the CF Provence whilst E332 resides in Switzerland at the Blonay-Chamby line near Montreux.

In 1914 the locomotives for which the Réseau Breton is best remembered arrived at Carhaix. These were the eight 0-6-6-0T Mallets built by Piguet of Lyon, (nos. E410-E417). Originally nine were ordered but the last of the batch failed to be completed due to the intervention of WW 1 These powerful locomotives, which weighed 54 Tonnes in working order, could haul 350 Tonne freight trains with ease and were the largest locomotives of their type in France. Their only restriction was that they were too heavy for use on the Châteaulin to Camaret line with its lighter track. Otherwise they were to be seen hauling heavy freight trains on the entire system until the metre gauge RB closed in 1967. Two of these impressive locomotives have survived as a reminder of their former exploits. E415 now stands on a plinth among flowerbeds close to Carhaix station whilst E 417 is in a private collection at Valence, having been stored for many years at Raucoules-Brossettes on the former Vivarais system. In order to confuse future historians, E417 carries the number E413 as a result of a last minute change of locomotives. E 413 had originally been selected by the purchaser, but found to have a broken piston valve. Rather than effect a repair, a simple exchange of identities was carried out!

In addition to the locomotives supplied directly to the RB, three additional machines were acquired from other lines in the years following WW 2. It will be noted that these late arrivals carried their original numbers, without the "E" (ETAT) prefix as used on the original stock. In 1944 a small SACM 2-4-0T(no.2504 -named *St Priest*), similar to the original RB locomotives, arrived from the CF de Cher whilst the following year a Corpet-Louvet 0-6-0T (no.107) was transferred from the CFDF. The most significant addition to the locomotive fleet occurred in 1953 when a Corpet-Louvet 0-6-6-0T Mallet (no.41) was transferred from the PO Corrèze. This impressive machine was built in 1913, one of five supplied to the CF du Centre. After a nomadic existence it arrived on the POC in 1947 but saw little service due to weight restrictions. Following arrival at Carhaix it remained in store until 1957 when it was finally overhauled and modified with a larger coal bunker. It then spent the next decade working freight trains between Loudéac and La Brohinière, making occasional visits to Carhaix for routine maintenance. Due to its smaller water carrying capacity, it was unsuited for use on the same rosters as the Piguet Mallets.

In 1936 the first railcar was supplied to the RB. This was a De Dion Bouton type NR (no. M1), fitted with a 150hp CLM 2-stroke engine. This proved to be unreliable and after two years was replaced by a 180hp Willeme unit. In 1940 the "NR" was transferred to the SE's Somme system after an order had been placed for six De Dion type OC2, a development of the OC1s supplied to the CdN in 1937. Due to the effects of WW 2, the OC2s (nos. X201-206) didn't arrive until 1946. With their 180hp Willeme power units, they proved most successful in service and continued in use until 1967 when they were transferred to the Blanc-Argent. No X205 remains in use at the BA whilst X202 has now returned to Brittany and is preserved by the CdN society at Langueux.

In 1951, three large Decauville type DXW railcars that had been intended for export to French Indo-China were transferred to Carhaix. Built in 1940, their delivery to the Far East had been prevented by the effects of WW 2 and remained in store at Corbeil. X231-233, with their twin Saurer 150hp power units, proved to be an excellent investment. With their extra power, they were suitable for hauling trailer cars, thus increasing their capacity. The trailer cars were in the form of seven Billard A-150-D units, which had their Willeme engines removed. Subsequently, three of the Billards were re-engined and became nos. X151-X153. Also in 1951, three early De Dion type NJ vehicles arrived from the SE Valmondois-Marines line and became M1-M3 on the RB. Their life at Carhaix was brief, being withdrawn between 1953 and 1957, although their Unic power units were retained as spares. One of the Decauville DXW units (X233) survives in store at Tence for future use on the Voies Ferrées du Velay along with Billard X153 and trailer car R5.

In 1956, the final railcars delivered to the RB arrived when the two De Dion Bouton Type OC1s were transferred from the CdN. Following overhaul at Carhaix, they emerged as nos. X157 and X158 and worked alongside their later sisters. As previously recorded, both have survived into preservation, the former at the Baie de Somme and the latter at the CdN society site at Langueux.

The passenger rolling stock comprised of a large fleet of wooden bodied bogie coaches with the usual end balconies. De Dietrich supplied 44 vehicles between 1891 and 1899, all consisting of a combination of first, second and third class accommodation. Between 1903 and 1911 a further 34 similar coaches were supplied by Carel. The last four were notable in being mounted on American style "Pennsylvania" sprung bogies in place of the older rigid types. These more luxurious vehicles were also fitted with toilets and fully upholstered seats. Intended for use on the yet to be built Camaret line, these coaches were known as the *"Baines de Mer"* type, although they were used throughout the entire system. The coaches with a guards and luggage compartment were sometimes equipped with a dog kennel. Access to these was by way of two small hatches on the outside of the bodywork.

With large and heavy freight traffic, the RB was equipped with a huge stock of wagons of many variations. These consisted of a combination of brake/luggage vans (fourgons), covered vans, open wagons, drop side wagons and bolster bogie wagons, all supplied at various times between 1891 and 1925. Many were equipped with vacuum braking equipment, particularly the covered vans, which were used primarily for the shellfish traffic from Camaret. The bogie wagons were built on the frames of withdrawn coaches, a common occurrence on many French lines.

Ten of the passenger coaches, including examples of both builders, have been preserved by the Chemin de Fer du Vivarais at Tournon. In addition the CFV has also saved the "Special Saloon" built by de Dietrich in 1899 and one of the fourgons. Other examples of RB rolling stock can be found at the CF de la Baie de Somme.

The Scene Today

Although the Réseau Breton in its original form closed in 1967, it is still possible to travel from Carhaix to Paimpol by train, albeit on standard gauge. With the notable exception of the final section between Pontrieux and Paimpol, with superb views of the Trieux estuary, the journey passes through a mainly rich agricultural landscape. Despite the lack of spectacular scenic attractions, it does convey an impression of the RB in its heyday, the station buildings and infrastructure having mainly remained unaltered.

Many of the old track beds are now footpaths, although some sections have been lost as a result of road improvement schemes. One notable survivor is the viaduct across the River Aulne at Châteaulin, which is now a very narrow, one-way traffic, road-bridge. Many former railway buildings have survived either as private dwellings or incorporated into industrial sites. Sadly some have been neglected and simply survive as shells, although their origin is still plain to see.

As one of the largest intensively used narrow gauge railways in France, it is a great tragedy that so little remains of the Réseau Breton. With foresight, some at least of the system could have been adapted as a tourist operation. The Camaret or Morlaix lines, with their attractive coastal destinations, would have been ideal candidates for such schemes. In 1967 railway preservation in France was in its infancy, consequently such imaginative plans were never considered.

Guingamp is situated on the SNCF line between Paris and Brest whilst Carhaix is located at the intersection of the D764 and N164 between Morlaix and Rennes. A regular daily service operates on the surviving standard gauge line between Carhaix, Guingamp and Paimpol. In addition an occasional steam hauled service operates during the summer on the scenic section between Paimpol and Pontrieux, utilising a former SNCF 4-6-0 as motive power.

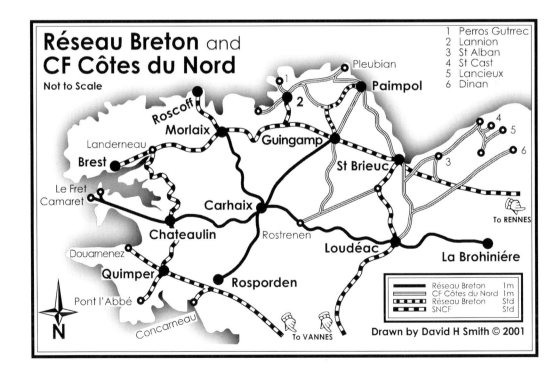

7.1. A Corpet-Louvet 0-6-0T of the CF Armoricains is seen at Morlaix. The viaduct in the background, was shared by the CF de l'ETAT and the Réseau Breton. It is now used by TGVs on the Paris to Brest service. (Coll - J.K.Williams).

7.2. Corpet-Louvet 0-6-0T no.106 of the CFA is at Primel in Finistère, with a large compliment of passengers. (Coll - J.K.Williams).

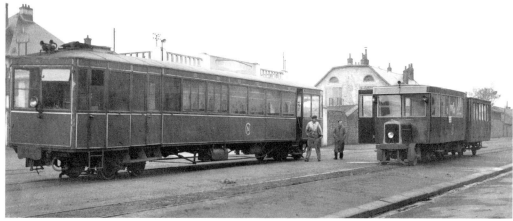

top left
7.3.   The impressive viaduct at Souzin is near St.Brieuc, on the CF des Côtes-du-Nord. This early view shows the junction of the lines to Paimpol and La Phare, the latter in the foreground. (Coll.- J.L.Rochaix / BVA).

left
7.4.   On the outskirts of St.Brieuc was another reinforced concrete viaduct. The Pont de Toupin was on the line to St.Cast whilst in the background can be seen the extensive buttressed viaducts leading into St.Brieuc Centrale station. (Coll.- P.Yvelin / BVA).

lower left
7.5.   The earliest locomotives on the CdN were the Blanc-Misseron 0-6-0Ts with fully enclosed wheels and motion. One of the last survivors was photographed in August 1946 at Etables between St.Brieuc and Paimpol. (J. Chapuis / BVA).

7.6.   The large Renault type NK railcar, known as Mamm-Goz, was recorded at St.Brieuc SNCF alongside one of the early De Dion Bouton type KG units in March 1946. (J. Chapuis / BVA).

7.7.   Shortly prior to the closure of the CdN, the RCTS organised a farewell special to this well loved system. Corpet-Louvet 0-6-0T no.39 prepares to depart from St.Brieuc SNCF on 25th August 1956. (D.Trevor Rowe).

7.8.   St.Brieuc Centrale had an impressive curved overall roof. A Renault ABH6 railcar stands at the platform in 1952. (B. Rozé / BVA).

7.9.   De Dion Bouton type OC1 railcar no.15 stands at St.Brieuc Centrale in 1955. Delivered to the CdN in 1937, these two successful vehicles remained in service until 1956. Following closure, they were transferred to the Réseau Breton. (R. Brugler / BVA).

top right
7.10.   Corpet-Louvet no.36 departs from St.Brieuc with a passenger train for Paimpol on 26th August 1956. This section of roadside track is built on one of the aforementioned buttressed viaducts. Although the CdN sadly closed in 1956, no.36 survived and is now preserved at Valmondois. (D.Trevor Rowe).

right
7.11.   One of the impressive Renault ABH6 railcars is seen at Binic between St.Brieuc and Paimpol in 1955. With closure only a year away, there was still a healthy patronage at this popular location on the coast. (R. Brugler / BVA).

lower right
7.12.   A freight train arrives at the busy port at Paimpol. In the background can be seen the two De Dion type OC1 railcars, both of which have been preserved. (J.Chapuis / BVA).

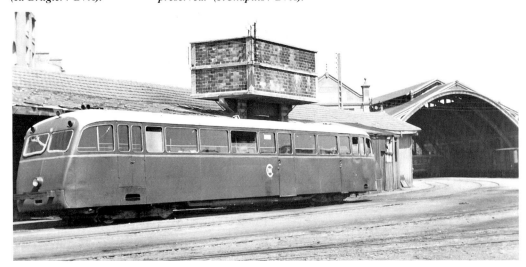

7.13.   At St.Brieuc-SNCF, Corpet-Louvet no.36 is turned alongside the platform at the end of its journey
from Paimpol. This scene dating from 1952 is so typical of the French narrow gauge railways.
(B. Rozé / BVA).

7.14.   This is an early view of Carhaix station on the Réseau Breton. One of the original batch of 2-4-0Ts
stands at the platform shortly after the opening of the line to Morlaix in 1891. (Coll. - Borderie / BVA).

7.15.   An almost identical view was photographed in 1954. One of the Decauville DXW railcars, with a Billard trailer car, arrives at the station with a train from Camaret. (M.Rifault.   Coll- J.L.Rochaix / BVA).

7.16.   A De Dion type OC2 railcar waits at Carhaix in August 1959. This scene has changed little at the present time except that the rails are now standard gauge. (J.B.Snell).

7.17.   At Morlaix, a De Dion railcar stands on the mixed gauge track alongside a SNCF diesel-electric locomotive on 16th May 1965. (B.Rozé / BVA).

7.18.   One of the Piguet 0-6-6-0T Mallets crosses the viaduct over the River Aulne at Châteaulin in 1967. This curved structure is now a very narrow road bridge. (A.Renault / BVA).

7.19.   Two Mallets pass at Callac with freight trains on the Carhaix to Guingamp line in September 1959. Heavy freight traffic was an everyday occurrence on the RB until its closure as a metre gauge system in 1967. (J.B.Snell).

7.20. Another Piguet Mallet storms through Mur de Bretagne on the line to Loudéac, shortly before closure, in August 1967. (A.Lepage / BVA).

7.21. The Corpet-Louvet 0-6-6-0T Mallet no.41 replenishes its water tanks at St.Lubin-Le-Vaublanc, between Loudéac and La Brohinière, on 7th November 1958. (B.Rozé / BVA).

7.22.   A Fives-Lille 4-6-0T hauls a short mixed train from Châteaulin to Carhaix in September 1958. The station building at St. Hernin is typical of the structures in this part of Brittany.   (J.B.Snell).

left
7.23. *Fives-Lille 4-6-0T no.332 leaves Camaret with the morning mixed train for Châteaulin on 27th August 1956. Camaret was, at that time, the most westerly station in France. (D.Trevor Rowe).*

lower left
7.24. *This Réseau Breton wooden bodied bogie coach built by Carel in 1911 contains a luggage and guards compartment. The two hatches at the far end are access to the dog kennels, which were incorporated in the luggage compartment. (J.L.Rochaix / BVA).*

7.25. *SACM 0-4-4-0T Mallet no. E 404, dating from 1894, is seen at Carhaix in 1957. Prior to the introduction of larger locomotives, these splendid machines handled most of the freight traffic and continued to haul mixed trains for many years. (B. Rozé / BVA).*

7.26. *Franco-Belge 4-6-0T no. E 325 was recorded at Carhaix depot in May 1960 following overhaul. These highly successful locomotives, along with the similar Fives-Lille variants, were the mainstay of locomotive haulage on the RB for over 60 years. (A. Renault / BVA).*

7.27. Equally synonymous with the Réseau Breton were the Piguet 0-6-6-0T Mallets. These impressive locomotives handled the majority of the heavy freight traffic following their introduction in 1914. No. E 414 is seen at Carhaix depot in 1954. (M.Rifault. Coll- J.L.Rochaix / BVA).

7.28. This scene emphases the intensive daily activities at the Réseau Breton. Two of the Piguet Mallets prepare for their duties at Carhaix depot on 17th June 1963. (J.L.Rochaix / BVA).

ENCORE

As recorded in the individual chapters of this book, many of the narrow gauge railways featured ceased to exist many years ago. Fortunately, some sections have survived as tourist operations, albeit very short remnants of the original systems in many cases. Although a tourist or museum line cannot faithfully replace the original railway as it operated in its heyday, they do at least convey a flavour of what was once an everyday scene throughout France. More importantly, they have preserved for posterity locomotives and rolling stock, which would otherwise have been reduced to scrap metal many years ago.

Details of the tourist railways featured can be obtained from the following addresses.

AMTP   Office de Tourisme, Rue Carnot, 45300 Pithiviers, France.
                             Tel: (0033) 02 38 30 50 02
CF de Saint-Eutrope   5 Square Montsouris, 75014 Paris, France.
                             Tel: (0033) 01 45 89 76 49
CF des Chanteraines   46 Avenue George Pompidou, 92390 Villeneuve-la-Garenne, Paris.
                             Tel: (0033) 01 40 85 86 20
APPEVA (Froissy-Cappy-Dompierre)
                             BP 106, 80001 Amiens Cedex 1, France.   Tel: (0033) 03 22 44 55 40
CF D'Abreschvillrer.   M.Gilbert Baillet,   Hotel des Cigognes, 57560 Abreschviller, France.
                             Tel: (0033) 03 87 03 79 12
CF du Blanc-Argent.   Gare de CFBA, 41200 Romorantin, France.
                             Tel: (0033) 02 54 76 06 51
CF de la Baie d Somme.   BP 31, 80230 St.Valery-sur-Somme, France.
                             Tel: (0033) 03 22 26 96 96
MTVS (Valmondois)   Mairie, 95430 Butry sur Oise, France.   Tel: (0033) 01 34 73 04 40

FURTHER READING

A number of books have been written about the French Narrow Gauge Railways, many of which are sadly currently out of print. The publications currently available are listed below. The monumental work by Keith Davies should be regarded as the definitive book on the subject.

MINOR RAILWAYS OF FRANCE   W.J.K.Davies   Plateway Press 2000
RAILWAYS OF THE BAIE DE SOMME   Philip Pacey   Oakwood Press 2000
RÉSEAU BRETON   Gordon Gravett   Oakwood Press. 1999
TOURIST RAILWAYS OF FRANCE   Richard Haworth   Rapid Transit Publications 1996
THE DECAUVILLE RAILWAYS   W.J.K.Davies   Narrow Gauge World Issues 9-14
NARROW GAUGE AT WAR (Part 1/ 2)   Keith Taylorson   Plateway Press 1996
THE LIGHT TRACK FROM ARRASS   T.R.Heritage   Plateway Press 1997

OF RELATED INTEREST

RAILWAYS TO VICTORY 1944-46   Vic Mitchell   Middleton Press 1998
VIVARAIS NARROW GAUGE   John Organ   Middleton Press 1999
SOUTHERN FRANCE NARROW GAUGE   John Organ   Middleton Press 2000
TRAMWAYS À VAPEUR DU TARN   Sarah Wright   Oakwood Press 2001

MP Middleton Press

Easebourne Lane, Midhurst, W Sussex. GU29 9AZ Tel: 01730 813169 Fax: 01730 812601
*If books are not available from your local transport stockist, order direct with cheque,
Visa or Mastercard, post free UK.*

BRANCH LINES

Branch Line to Allhallows
Branch Line to Alton
Branch Lines around Ascot
Branch Lines to Ashburton
Branch Lines around Bodmin
Branch Line to Bude
Branch Lines around Canterbury
Branch Lines around Chard & Yeovil
Branch Line to Cheddar
Branch Lines around Cromer
Branch Lines to East Grinstead
Branch Lines of East London
Branch Lines to Effingham Junction
Branch Lines around Exmouth
Branch Lines to Falmouth, Helston & St. Ives
Branch Line to Fairford
Branch Lines around Gosport
Branch Line to Hawkhurst
Branch Lines to Horsham
Branch Lines around Huntingdon
Branch Line to Ilfracombe
Branch Line to Kingswear
Branch Line to Lambourn
Branch Lines to Launceston & Princetown
Branch Line to Looe
Branch Line to Lyme Regis
Branch Lines around Midhurst
Branch Line to Minehead
Branch Line to Moretonhampstead
Branch Lines to Newport
Branch Lines to Newquay
Branch Lines around North Woolwich
Branch Line to Padstow
Branch Lines around Plymouth
Branch Lines to Seaton and Sidmouth
Branch Line to Selsey
Branch Lines around Sheerness
Branch Line to Shrewsbury
Branch Line to Swanage *updated*
Branch Line to Tenterden
Branch Lines around Tiverton
Branch Lines to Torrington
Branch Lines to Tunbridge Wells
Branch Line to Upwell
Branch Lines of West London
Branch Lines around Weymouth
Branch Lines around Wimborne
Branch Lines around Wisbech

NARROW GAUGE

Branch Line to Lynton
Branch Lines around Portmadoc 1923-46
Branch Lines around Porthmadog 1954-94
Branch Line to Southwold
Douglas to Port Erin
Kent Narrow Gauge
Northern France Narrow Gauge
Romneyrail
Southern France Narrow Gauge
Sussex Narrow Gauge
Two-Foot Gauge Survivors
Vivarais Narrow Gauge

SOUTH COAST RAILWAYS

Ashford to Dover
Bournemouth to Weymouth
Brighton to Worthing
Eastbourne to Hastings
Hastings to Ashford
Portsmouth to Southampton
Ryde to Ventnor
Southampton to Bournemouth

SOUTHERN MAIN LINES

Basingstoke to Salisbury
Bromley South to Rochester
Crawley to Littlehampton
Dartford to Sittingbourne
East Croydon to Three Bridges
Epsom to Horsham
Exeter to Barnstaple
Exeter to Tavistock
Faversham to Dover
London Bridge to East Croydon
Orpington to Tonbridge
Tonbridge to Hastings
Salisbury to Yeovil
Swanley to Ashford
Tavistock to Plymouth
Three Bridges to Brighton
Victoria to Bromley South
Victoria to East Croydon
Waterloo to Windsor
Waterloo to Woking
Woking to Portsmouth
Woking to Southampton
Yeovil to Exeter

EASTERN MAIN LINES

Ely to Kings Lynn
Fenchurch Street to Barking
Ipswich to Saxmundham
Liverpool Street to Ilford
Saxmundham to Yarmouth

WESTERN MAIN LINES

Ealing to Slough
Exeter to Newton Abbot
Newton Abbot to Plymouth
Newbury to Westbury
Paddington to Ealing
Plymouth to St. Austell
Slough to Newbury
St. Austell to Penzance

COUNTRY RAILWAY ROUTES

Andover to Southampton
Bath Green Park to Bristol
Bath to Evercreech Junction
Bournemouth to Evercreech Jn.
Cheltenham to Andover
Croydon to East Grinstead
Didcot to Winchester
East Kent Light Railway
Fareham to Salisbury

Guildford to Redhill
Reading to Basingstoke
Reading to Guildford
Redhill to Ashford
Salisbury to Westbury
Stratford upon Avon to Cheltenham
Strood to Paddock Wood
Taunton to Barnstaple
Wenford Bridge to Fowey
Westbury to Bath
Woking to Alton
Yeovil to Dorchester

GREAT RAILWAY ERAS

Ashford from Steam to Eurostar
Clapham Junction 50 years of change
Festiniog in the Fifties
Festiniog in the Sixties
Isle of Wight Lines 50 years of change
Railways to Victory 1944-46
Return to Blaenau 1970-82
SECR Centenary album
Talyllyn 50 years of change
Yeovil 50 years of change

LONDON SUBURBAN RAILWAYS

Caterham and Tattenham Corner
Charing Cross to Dartford
Clapham Jn. to Beckenham Jn.
Crystal Palace (HL) & Catford Loop
East London Line
Finsbury Park to Alexandra Palace
Kingston and Hounslow Loops
Lewisham to Dartford
Lines around Wimbledon
London Bridge to Addiscombe
Mitcham Junction Lines
North London Line
South London Line
West Croydon to Epsom
West London Line
Willesden Junction to Richmond
Wimbledon to Beckenham
Wimbledon to Epsom

STEAMING THROUGH

Steaming through Cornwall
Steaming through the Isle of Wight
Steaming through Kent
Steaming through West Hants
Steaming through West Sussex

TRAMWAY CLASSICS

Aldgate & Stepney Tramways
Barnet & Finchley Tramways
Bath Tramways
Brighton's Tramways
Bristol's Tramways
Burton & Ashby Tramways
Camberwell & W.Norwood Tramways
Clapham & Streatham Tramways
Croydon's Tramways

Dover's Tramways
East Ham & West Ham Tramways
Edgware and Willesden Tramways
Eltham & Woolwich Tramways
Embankment & Waterloo Tramways
Enfield & Wood Green Tramways
Exeter & Taunton Tramways
Greenwich & Dartford Tramways
Hammersmith & Hounslow Tramways
Hampstead & Highgate Tramways
Hastings Tramways
Holborn & Finsbury Tramways
Ilford & Barking Tramways
Kingston & Wimbledon Tramways
Lewisham & Catford Tramways
Liverpool Tramways 1. Eastern Routes
Liverpool Tramways 2. Southern Routes
Liverpool Tramways 3. Northern Routes
Maidstone & Chatham Tramways
Margate to Ramsgate
North Kent Tramways
Norwich Tramways
Portsmouth's Tramways
Reading Tramways
Seaton & Eastbourne Tramways
Shepherds Bush & Uxbridge Tramways
Southampton Tramways
Southend-on-sea Tramways
Southwark & Deptford Tramways
Stamford Hill Tramways
Twickenham & Kingston Tramways
Victoria & Lambeth Tramways
Waltham Cross & Edmonton Tramways
Walthamstow & Leyton Tramways
Wandsworth & Battersea Tramways

TROLLEYBUS CLASSICS

Bournemouth Trolleybuses
Croydon Trolleybuses
Derby Trolleybuses
Hastings Trolleybuses
Maidstone Trolleybuses
Portsmouth Trolleybuses
Reading Trolleybuses
Woolwich & Dartford Trolleybuses

WATERWAY ALBUMS

Kent and East Sussex Waterways
London to Portsmouth Waterway
West Sussex Waterways

MILITARY BOOKS

Battle over Portsmouth
Battle over Sussex 1940
Bombers over Sussex 1943-45
Bognor at War
Military Defence of West Sussex
Military Signals from the South Coast
Secret Sussex Resistance
Surrey Home Guard

OTHER RAILWAY BOOKS

Index to all Middleton Press stations
Industrial Railways of the South-
South Eastern & Chatham Railway
London Chatham & Dover Railway
War on the Line (SR 1939-45)

BIOGRAPHIES

Garraway Father & Son
Mitchell & company